THE COMPLETE GUIDELINES TO IMPROVISATION FOR PIANO VOL. 1-3

By Marvin Kahn

VOLUME 1	VOLUME 2	VOLUME 3
3	42	82

ORIGINAL PHOTO COURTESY OF STEINWAY & SONS

COVER XEROGRAPHY TY OCHMAN
ART DIRECTION/DESIGN TY OCHMAN

INTRODUCTION

The complete Guidelines to Improvisation combines Volumes 1, 2 and 3 of the successful series into one giant treatise on improvisation for the piano.

The series was designed for the student, who, having learned the rudiments of music in the usual course of piano instruction, is now ready to discover all the joys of self-expression in popular piano playing.

In **Volume 1**, the student will learn how to construct Major, Minor, Diminished and Augmented Triads, and how to build them upon each of the 12 tones of the chromatic scale. (In both root position and inversions). Various types of bass patterns are introduced, and are correlated with written drills, as are chords of the added sixth and dominant seventh.

To reinforce the studies, drills and bass patterns, arrangements of well-known standards, such as "I'm Forever Blowing Bubbles" and "Zing! Went the Strings of My Heart," are included, illustrating each topic. Original compositions by Marvin Kahn are also included, along with popular folk songs such as "Molly Malone" and "Go Tell It On The Mountain."

Volume 2 concentrates on Seventh Chord formations; and the beginning of style is taught through the use of left hand bass patterns for waltz and fox-trot tempos. Popular waltzes such as "Fascination," "For You," and "Till We Meet Again" are used as illustrations and drills. Fox-trot illustrations include "Pretty Baby," "Too Marvelous For Words," "April Showers," and "Autumn In New York."

Volume 3 presents 9th, 11th, 13th and suspended 4th chords, as used in both harmonization and melodic improvisation. Pedal point is discussed, and the art of playing from a lead sheet is explained. The analyses presented in this volume will give the student the freedom to play instantly any pop song from chord symbols, regardless of tempo, chord structure or melody. All technical material is given immediate practical application, and is fully illustrated with such great standard songs as "The Days of Wine and Roses," "Body and Soul," "April In Paris," and many others.

Part I

Chord Structure	4
Triads	4
Major Triad Structure	4
Chord Symbols	5
Improvisation on Major Triads	7
Minor Triad Structure	11
Runs (Arpeggios)	11
Fill-ins	13
Diminished Triad Structure	16
Augmented Triad Structure	17
Summary of Triad Tables	20

Part II

Chord Inversions	21
How to Name a Chord Inversion	22
The Dominant Seventh Structure	25
Open Position Triads	27
Added Sixth Chords	32

Part III

Flat Chords	36
First Group	36
Second Group	37
Third Group	37
Summary of Flat Triads	38

Songs

Put On Your Old Grey Bonnet	6
I Like Mountain Music	9
My Wild Irish Rose	13
Cockles & Mussels	15
Blues Lament	17
Melody	19
Go Tell It On The Mountain	23
I'm Forever Blowing Bubbles	29
Kind-a-Moody	55
Busy Neighbors	57
The Japanese Sandman	59
For You	63
Till We Meet Again	67
Fascination	69
Pretty Baby	72
Too Marvelous For Words	74
April Showers	76
Autumn In New York	80

PART I.

CHORD STRUCTURE

One of the chief prerequisites of popular piano playing is the ability to improvise a *pleasing* background to a melody. By "pleasing" we mean harmonious, and Harmony may be looked upon as the science of <u>chords</u>. A chord is a group of three or more tones, harmonically ("pleasingly") related, which are sounded simultaneously. The simplest of these, the three-tone chord, is called a <u>triad</u>.

TRIADS

Triads may be built upon any tone, which is thus called its <u>root.</u> The middle tone is called the <u>third,</u> and the top tone the <u>fifth.</u> Each triad is named for its root.

Triads are the basis of all larger chords, and from them we derive changes in *quality*. The first *quality* is <u>Major</u>.

MAJOR TRIAD STRUCTURE

The Major Triad consists of the first (root), third, and fifth degrees (notes) of the major scale based on the same root. The interval between the root and third must be a "major third" (four half-steps), and the interval between the third and fifth a "minor third" (three half-steps).

The following is a Table of Major Triads built on the white notes of the keyboard:

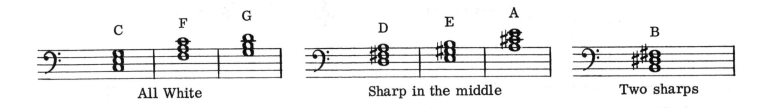

Notice that "D," "E," and "A" Major Triads have a sharp in the middle to conform to the interval structure required for Major Triads. It is for the same reason that the "B" Major Triad has *two* sharps.

Thus, the ALL-WHITE major triads are:

C (CEG), F (FAC), and G (GBD)

The SHARP-IN-THE-MIDDLE major triads are:

D (DF♯A), E (EG♯B), and A (AC♯E).

B has *two* sharps (BD♯F♯).

Let us transfer this into another image, this time visualizing white (☐) and black (■) keys.

Visual Table of Major Triads

C = ☐☐☐   D = ☐■☐   B = ☐■■

F = ☐☐☐   E = ☐■☐

G = ☐☐☐   A = ☐■☐

Play the following example. The left hand chords are all *major triads*, and the symbols are placed under the chords for easier understanding.

CHORD SYMBOLS

On a popular song sheet the name of the chord may be found by referring to the chord symbol above the melody in the singer's part (top staff) or, in some cases, above the guitar frame, viz.:

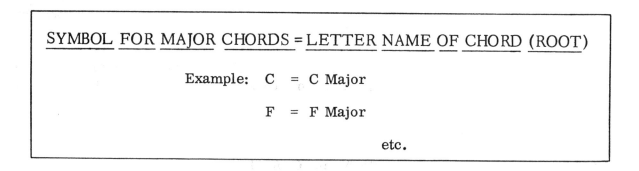

Now play PUT ON YOUR OLD GREY BONNET using the chords in the left hand as indicated by the chord symbols on the lower staff.

PUT ON YOUR OLD GREY BONNET

Words by
STANLEY MURPHY

Music by
PERCY WENRICH

Put On Your Old Grey Bon - net with the

blue rib - bon on it, While I hitch old Dob - bin to the shay,

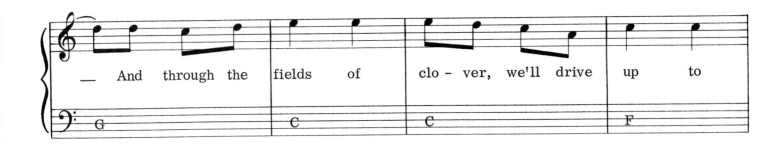

_ And through the fields of clo - ver, we'll drive up to

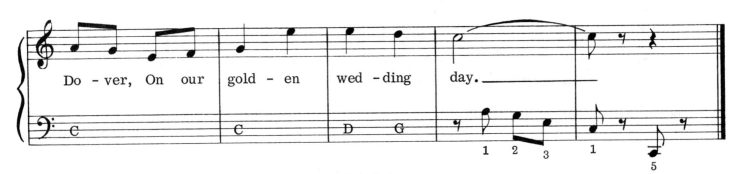

Do - ver, On our gold - en wed - ding day.

DRILL: Name and play the following triads:

Examples:

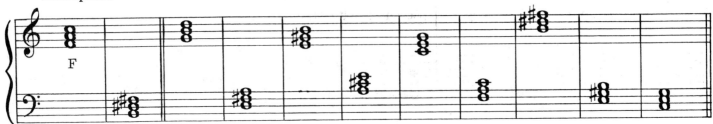

IMPROVISATION ON MAJOR TRIADS

Many bass patterns may be evolved from any chord. Let us explore several based on the Major Triad. This is the simplest form of left hand improvisation.

Broken Chord in 2/4

Our first bass pattern is the <u>Broken Chord</u> which consists of the single note *root* followed by the *third* and *fifth* of the chord played simultaneously.

Examples:

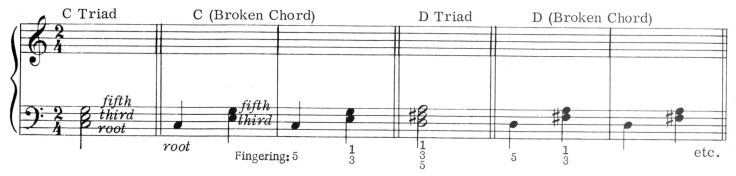

Using the Broken Chord pattern, play PUT ON YOUR OLD GREY BONNET as shown on page 4. (The third measure from the end, which has two chords, should be played "block style," i.e., holding the chords, inasmuch as two chords occur in this measure.) Play the ending as given.

Alberti Bass in 2/4

A second bass pattern consists of single notes played in the following order: *root, fifth, third, fifth*. This is called <u>Alberti Bass</u>, having been invented by Alberti, an early Italian composer.

Example:

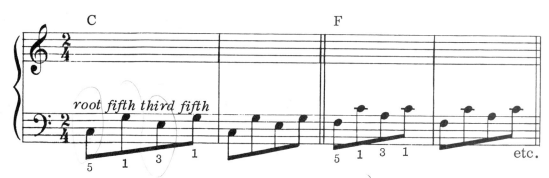

Using the Alberti Bass for PUT ON YOUR OLD GREY BONNET, it would appear as follows:

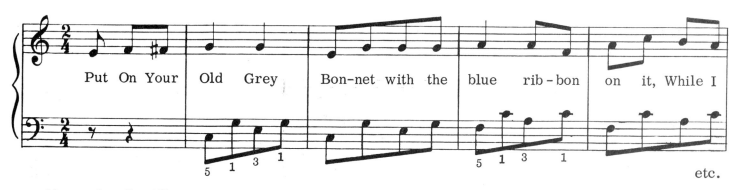

Now using the Alberti Bass play PUT ON YOUR OLD GREY BONNET as shown on page 5, again playing "block style" at the "D G" measure.

Most popular songs are either in $\frac{4}{4}$ meter (sometimes called "Common Time," for which the time signature is **C**), or *alla breve* (known as "Cut Time," indicated by the sign **¢**). In both cases, accompaniment may be improvised as follows:

Broken Chord in $\frac{4}{4}$

Alberti Bass in $\frac{4}{4}$

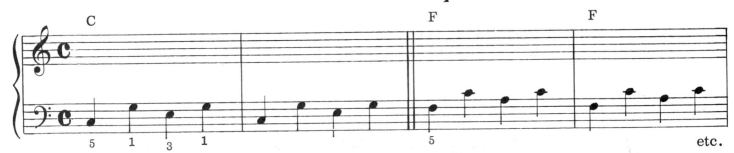

In the following song, I LIKE MOUNTAIN MUSIC, use the following procedure:

1) Play using chords in left hand held for a full measure.
2) Play using the Broken Chord accompaniment.
3) Play using the Alberti Bass.

Examples of Accompaniment

1. Full Chords

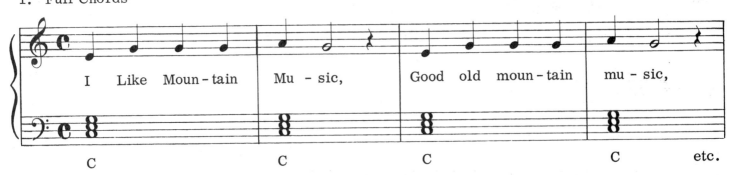

2. Broken Chord

3. Alberti Bass

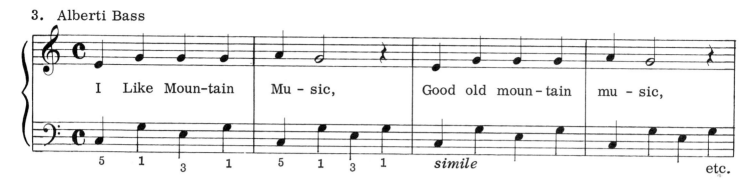

I Like Moun-tain Mu - sic, Good old moun - tain mu - sic,

simile   etc.

Now let us combine the various accompaniments into one complete arrangement of I LIKE MOUN-TAIN MUSIC. Section A will be played with the Alberti Bass; Section B with Broken Chords excepting where "block chords" are indicated at the 7th and 8th measures; and Section C with the Alberti Bass, excepting the 5th and 6th measures, where chords are indicated on the offbeat. At Section D return to Broken Chords. When you have mastered this routine, try your hand at doing things *your way*. Take the different bass patterns you have learned and mix them up any way you like. Remember, a fine popular pianist almost *never* plays a piece the same way twice.

I LIKE MOUNTAIN MUSIC

Words by
JAMES CAVANAUGH

Music by
FRANK WELDON

A Alberti Bass

I Like Moun-tain Mu - sic, Good old moun -tain mu - sic, Played by a

B Broken Chords

real hill-bil - ly band.____ Give me ru - ral rhy - thm,

Let me sway right with 'em; I think their mel-o-dies are grand.__ I've heard Ha-

C   C   G   G   C F   C

chord chord chord

C Alberti Bass

wai - ians play, From the land of the wick - y wack - y; But

F   F   F   C

I must say That they can't beat the "Tur-key in the straw", by crack-y!

G D   G G   D   G

chord chord chord chord   chord   chord

D Broken Chords

I Like Moun - tain Mu - sic, good old moun - tain mu - sic,

C   C   C   C

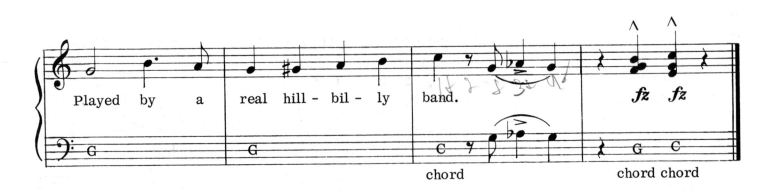

Played by a real hill-bil-ly band.

fz fz

G   G   C   G C

chord   chord chord

MINOR TRIAD STRUCTURE

The second *quality* is the <u>Minor</u>.   To form a Minor Triad lower the third of the Major Chord one half-step.   The lower interval, root to third, will be a "minor third" (three half-steps).   The upper interval, third to fifth, becomes a "major third" (four half-steps).

The following is a Table of Minor Triads built on the white notes of the keyboard:

FLAT - IN - THE - MIDDLE   ALL WHITE   ONE SHARP

Visual Table of Minor Triads

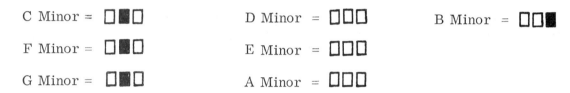

<u>KEYBOARD DRILL:</u>

Play the C, F, G, D, A, E, and B chords cross-hand full chord, first as Major, then as Minor as shown in the following example for the C chords:

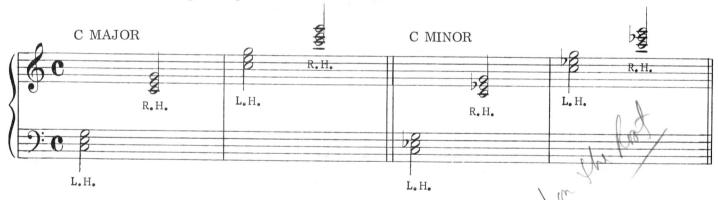

RUNS (ARPEGGIOS)

A <u>run</u> is a term used for an <u>arpeggio,</u> or the playing of the notes of a chord one after the other (broken), rather than together (blocked).

<u>KEYBOARD DRILL:</u>

Play the C, F, G, D, A, E, and B triads as cross-hand runs (arpeggios) for Major and Minor as shown in the following example:

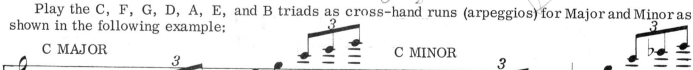

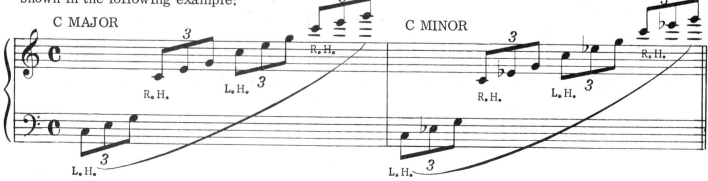

12

> MINOR CHORD SYMBOL = Root plus "m" or "mi"
> (depending upon the publisher)
>
> Example: Cm = C Minor
>
>   Gmi = G Minor   etc.

DRILL:

Name and play the following chords and arpeggios.   They will be either Major or Minor.

Examples:

Arpeggiated Chord in 3/4

Chords (triads) played as arpeggios in 3/4 would appear as in this example:

Broken Chord in 3/4

The following is the formula for the Broken Chord (triad) in 3/4 meter:

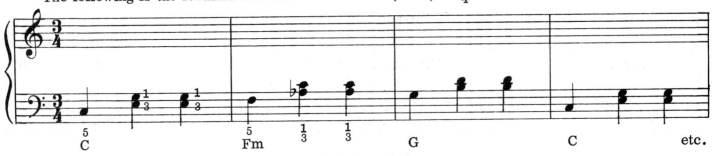

FILL - INS

Whenever there is a long wait in the melody, it is necessary to invent or "fill in" a melodic idea. A simple <u>fill-in</u> is illustrated in the last two measures of the following quotation from MY WILD I-RISH ROSE. Throughout this book all fill-ins will be written out.

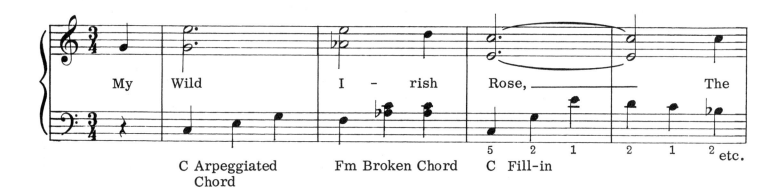

Now try out what you have just learned about $\frac{3}{4}$ bass patterns by making a complete arrangement of that lovely old standard waltz, MY WILD IRISH ROSE. First play the bass patterns called for at sections A , B , and C. Then try switching them around, or changing every two measures, whatever sounds best to *you*. Remember, we are trying to help *you* learn how to express your*self*. And above all, *do not write in the left hand part*. The first step to improvisation is the ability to play what is *not printed*.

MY WILD IRISH ROSE

Words and Music by
CHANUCEY OLCOTT

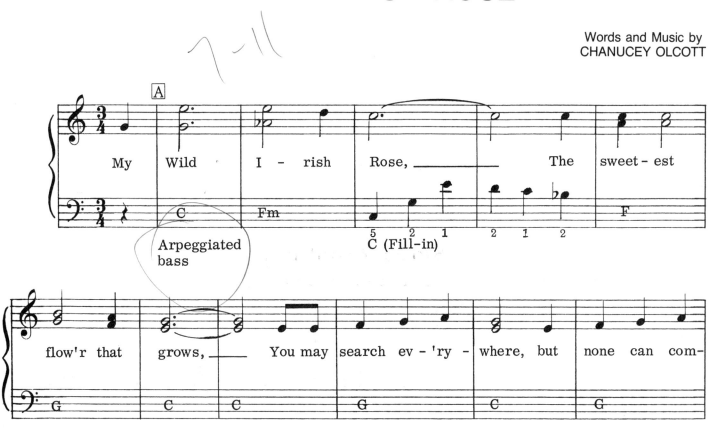

14

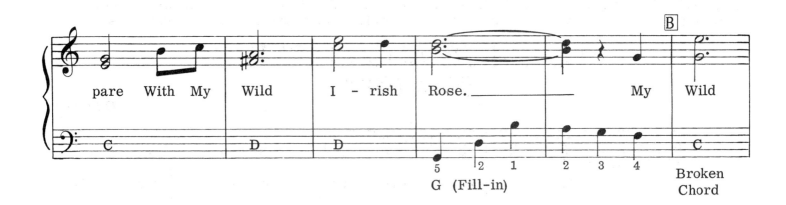

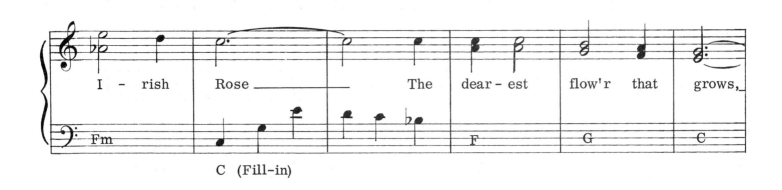

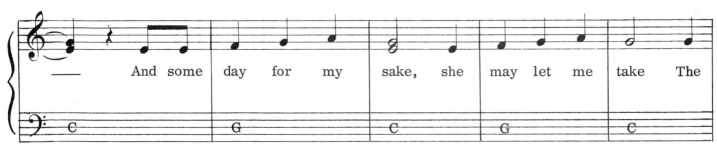

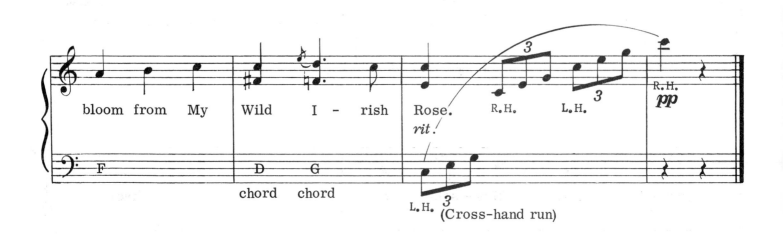

Now try making your own arrangement of COCKLES AND MUSSELS ("Molly Malone"). Be careful to make the changes between the Major and Minor chords. Where more than one chord occurs in a measure, it is best at this stage to play full block chord style; that is, holding the chords.

COCKLES AND MUSSELS
(Molly Malone)

Old Irish Air

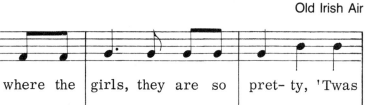

In Dub - lin Cit - y where the girls, they are so pret- ty, 'Twas

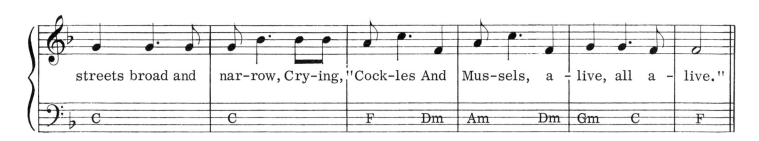

there I first met with sweet Mol - ly Ma - lone; She drove a wheel -bar-row, thro'

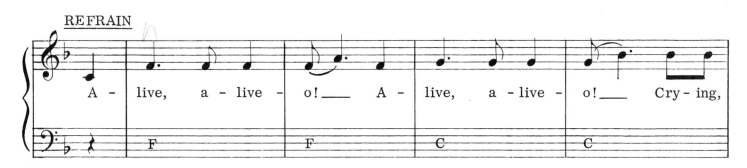

streets broad and nar-row, Cry-ing, "Cock-les And Mus-sels, a - live, all a - live."

REFRAIN

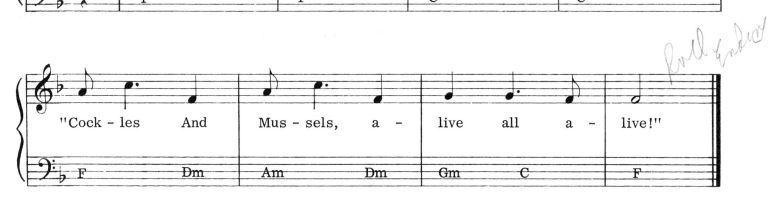

A - live, a - live - o!___ A - live, a - live - o!___ Cry - ing,

"Cock - les And Mus - sels, a - live all a - live!"

DIMINISHED TRIAD STRUCTURE

The third *quality* is the <u>Diminished</u>. The Diminished Triad consists of two "minor thirds" (three half-steps each, of course). To form a Diminished Triad, take the Minor Triad and lower the fifth tone one half-step. For example:

| F Minor | F Diminished | G Minor | G Diminished | C Minor | C Diminished etc. |

Visual Table of Diminished Triads

C Diminished = ▢■■   D Diminished = ▢▢■   B Diminished = ▢▢▢

F Diminished = ▢■▢   E Diminished = ▢▢■

G Diminished = ▢■■   A Diminished = ▢▢■

<u>KEYBOARD DRILL:</u>

Play the C, F, G, D, A, E, and B Triads as cross-hand arpeggios ("runs") for Major, Minor, and Diminished *qualities*.

DIMINISHED CHORD SYMBOL = Root plus "o" or "dim"

Example: C° = C Diminished

G dim = G Diminished   etc.

<u>DRILL:</u>

Name and play the following chords and arpeggios using the proper symbols. They will be Major, Minor, or Diminished.

Examples:

Play the next composition, BLUES LAMENT, holding the bass as all block chords. Play the G chord 𝄢 in this register. All left hand chords except the last measure should be sustained for two beats.

BLUES LAMENT

By MARVIN KAHN

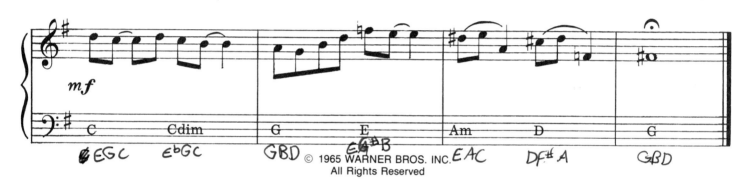

Because the Diminished Chord is seldom played as a triad,* let us now move to the fourth *quality*, namely: the <u>Augmented</u>.

AUGMENTED TRIAD STRUCTURE

To *augment* something means to make it *larger*. When we make a chord *augmented*, it is *larger* than Major. To form an Augmented Triad, then, take the Major Triad and *raise* the fifth (top) tone one half-step.

Example:

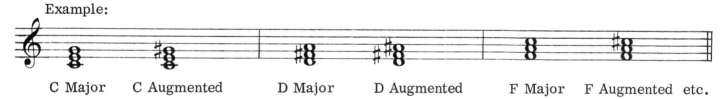

C Major   C Augmented   D Major   D Augmented   F Major   F Augmented etc.

Visual Table of Augmented Triads

C Augmented = ☐☐■   D Augmented = ☐■■   B Augmented = ☐■☐

F Augmented = ☐☐■   E Augmented = ☐■☐

G Augmented = ☐☐■   A Augmented = ☐■☐

* Book II of this course discusses the Diminished Seventh Chord, which enhances the Diminished *quality*.

KEYBOARD DRILL:

Play the C, F, G, D, E, A, and B triads as cross-hand arpeggios ("runs") for Major, Minor, Diminished, and Augmented *qualities* as shown in the following routine for C:

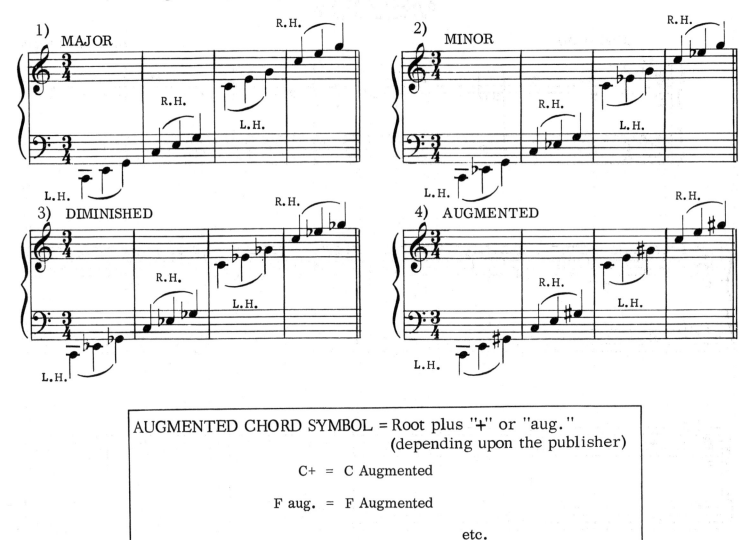

AUGMENTED CHORD SYMBOL = Root plus "+" or "aug."
                           (depending upon the publisher)

C+ = C Augmented

F aug. = F Augmented

etc.

DRILL:

Name and play the following chords and arpeggios. They will be Major, Minor, Diminished, or Augmented. Use the correct symbol for each *quality*.

Examples:

In the following composition, MELODY, three changes in *quality* are used. Play the left hand with the Arpeggiated $\frac{3}{4}$ Bass. The ending is a G cross-hand run and should be played as written.

MELODY

By MARVIN KAHN

G Cross-hand run

SUMMARY OF TRIADS TABLE

VISUAL SUMMARY OF TRIADS

(Root Position)

	MAJOR	MINOR	DIMINISHED	AUGMENTED
C =	□□□	□■□	□■■	□□■
F =	□□□	□■□	□■□	□□■
G =	□□□	□■□	□■■	□□■
D =	□■□	□□□	□□■	□■■
E =	□■□	□□□	□□■	□■□
A =	□■□	□□□	□□■	□■□
B =	□■■	□□■	□□□	□■□

CHORD INVERSIONS

A triad may be played with its notes rearranged in a different <u>position.</u>   When the triad is played with the root tone as the lowest note, it is in the <u>root position.</u>   So far in this book all triads have been played in root position.

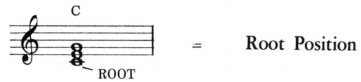

=   **Root Position**

When the *third* of the triad is the lowest tone, the chord is in the <u>first inversion.</u>

=   **First Inversion**

When the *fifth* of the chord is the lowest tone, the chord is in the second inversion.

=   **Second Inversion**

Below is the C Major Chord written in all inversions.   Practice this drill, hands separately:

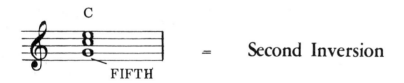

Triads may also be inverted for the other changes in *quality* such as Minor, Diminished, and Augmented. In popular music the Diminished and Augmented Inversions usually take the name of the lower tone. In this book, we will only be concerned with inversions of the Major and Minor Chords. For example:

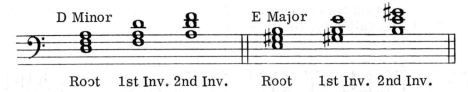

HOW TO NAME A CHORD INVERSION

All triads are built in thirds and appear on the staff as line-line-line, or space-space-space. When a triad is inverted, this sequence is broken. The first note that is *not* in a sequence of thirds (from bottom to top) is the *name* of the chord (or the <u>root</u>).

Example:

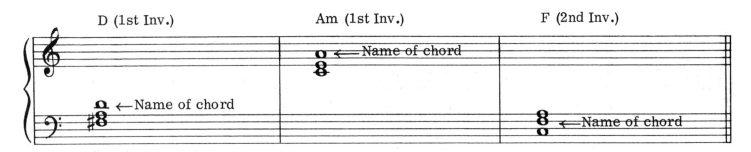

<u>DRILL:</u>

Name and play the chords below and indicate their inversions. The symbols for First Inversion is a small "1" placed next to the letter name; for the Second Inversion a small "2". If in root position just use the letter name.

Examples:

The next song, GO TELL IT ON THE MOUNTAIN, is an American folk spiritual. The left hand chords will be played "block style" (held), using inversions.

First play it as written out on this page. Then play it as per page 23, supplying *root positions* and *inversions* as called for by the symbols.

GO TELL IT ON THE MOUNTAIN

American Folk Song

GO TELL IT ON THE MOUNTAIN

American Folk Song

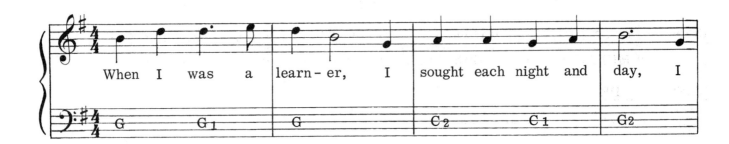

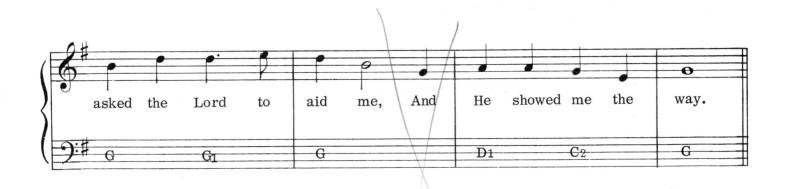

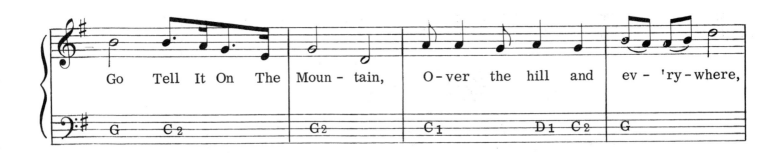

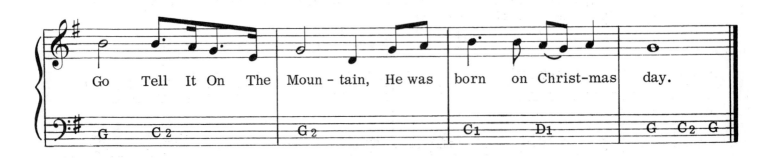

THE DOMINANT SEVENTH STRUCTURE

Seventh Chords are triads with a fourth harmony note added. The most common of these, and the only one we will discuss in this book, is the Dominant Seventh, consisting of a *major triad* plus a *minor third*.

Example:

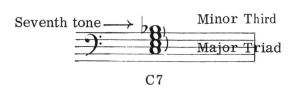

Note: The *seventh* of the chord is *one whole step* (or two half-steps) *below* the *octave*.

FORMULA: root, third, fifth, seventh (one whole step below octave)

KEYBOARD DRILL:

Play the following Dominant Sevenths:

L.H. fingering = 5321*

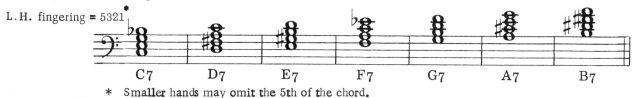

C7 D7 E7 F7 G7 A7 B7

* Smaller hands may omit the 5th of the chord.

DOMINANT SEVENTH CHORD SYMBOL = Root plus "7"

Example:

G_7 = G Dominant Seventh (GBDF)

D_7 = D Dominant Seventh (DF♯AC)   etc.

Most Dominant Sevenths in this book will be played in root position, but C_7 nearly always will be played in the second inversion:

1
2
3
5

In the following waltz, I'M FOREVER BLOWING BUBBLES, all triads and seventh chords will be played in root position, except for C and C7 which will be played in the second inversion. These are the chords used in this song. Practice them well!

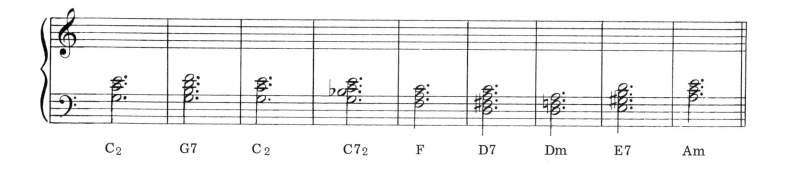

C₂   G7   C₂   C7₂   F   D7   Dm   E7   Am

I'M FOREVER BLOWING BUBBLES

Words and Music by
JAAN KENBROVIN and JOHN WILLIAM KELLETTE

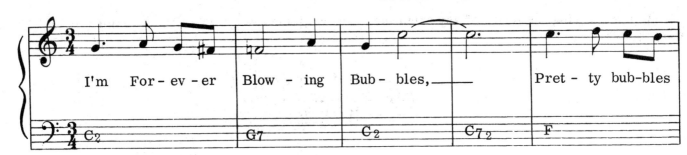

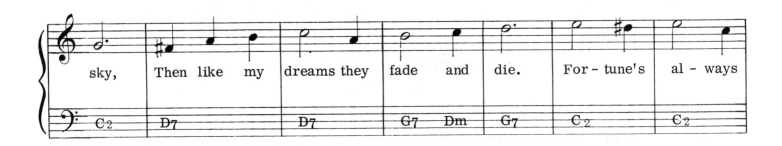

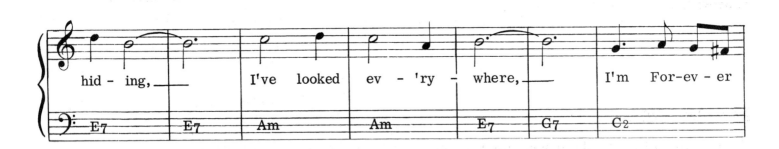

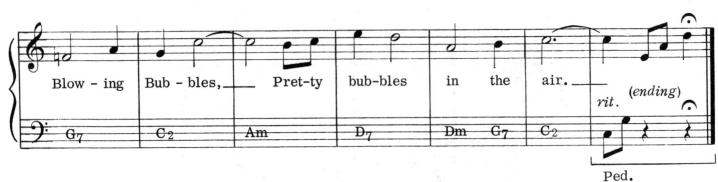

OPEN POSITION TRIADS

By rearranging the tones of any triad they may be played in open position.   Here is the triad in close position:

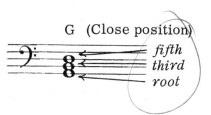

By moving the third of the triad to the top an open position is achieved. The third is now two tones above the octave and is called the <u>tenth</u>.   The pattern is: *root, fifth, third* (or *tenth*).

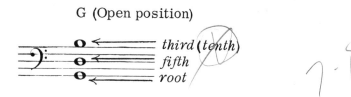

(Try "opening up" some triads of your own.)

Open Position Bass in ¾
("Broken 5 and 10")

Using the formula root, fifth, third (or tenth), a fine accompaniment may be played. This formula applies to all changes in *quality*, but in this book it will be used for Major and Minor only.   Because it is an Arpeggiated or Broken Chord using the fifth and tenth, we call it the "<u>Broken 5 and 10</u>," which abbreviated becomes "Br. 5 & 10".

<u>KEYBOARD DRILL</u>:

Play the following Major and Minor patterns for D, E, F, G, A, and B Triads.

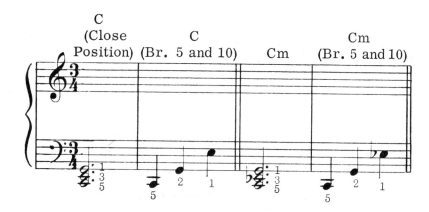

In the following arrangement of I'M FOREVER BLOWING BUBBLES, where no other indication is given, play all the chords in the left hand using the "Broken 5 and 10 Bass." The fill-ins and the ending are written out. When a chord is written with the word STOP underneath, it means to play the full "block chord" and hold for the duration of time indicated. To get you started, the first three "Broken 5 and 10" bars are written out.

I'M FOREVER BLOWING BUBBLES

Words and Music by
JAAN KENBROVIN and JOHN WILLIAM KELLETTE

Review of Left Hand Accompaniments and Patterns in $\frac{3}{4}$

Thus far the following left hand patterns in $\frac{3}{4}$ meter have been introduced:

1. BROKEN CHORD

C

2. ARPEGGIATED CHORD

C

3. STOP CHORD, ROOT POSITION

C

4. STOP CHORD, INVERSIONS

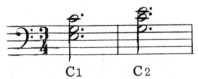

C1   C2

5. STOP CHORD FOR THE DOMINANT SEVENTH

C7

6. "BROKEN 5 AND 10" (OPEN POSITION TRIADS)

C

Now try to make your own arrangement of the waltz, MEMORIES, using these patterns in the left hand. Any type of bass pattern should be used for *at least two measures*. Do not introduce too many styles of accompaniment in one song, as it becomes cluttered.

SUGGESTIONS:

(1) When two chords appear in one measure, it is wise to play them as stop (block) chords. One new chord, the F♯7, appears and is written out.

(2) If you wish to use the open position for a seventh chord, treat the chord as a triad, omit the third, and add the seventh. A seventh chord played block style should, of course include the seventh tone.

(3) Most block chords sound best in the register of five notes below and above Middle C.

Open Seventh Formula = root, fifth, seventh

G7 (open position)

Fingering: 5   2   1

root   fifth   seventh

MEMORIES

Words by
GUSTAVE KAHN

Music by
EGBERT VAN ALSTYNE

ADDED SIXTH CHORDS

Major and minor triads may be enriched by adding a fourth tone to form a Sixth Chord. This added tone is *one whole step* above the fifth of the triad.

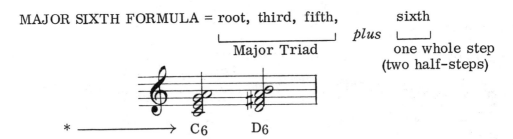

MAJOR SIXTH FORMULA = root, third, fifth, *plus* sixth
Major Triad
one whole step
(two half-steps)

C6   D6

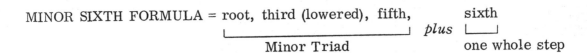

MINOR SIXTH FORMULA = root, third (lowered), fifth, *plus* sixth
Minor Triad
one whole step

Em6   Fm6

* (Notice the self-explanatory chord symbols)

NOTE: The Sixth Chord is very effective as an ending, particularly if played as an arpeggiated run.

Example:

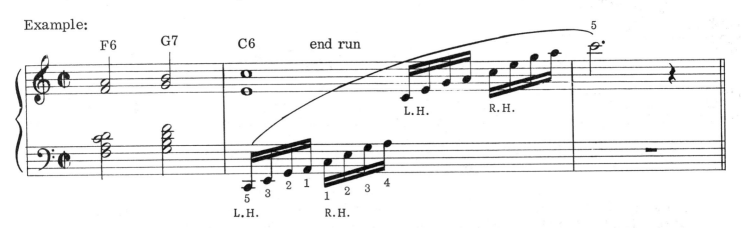

Lower Neighbors

A lower neighbor is a tone used *with* a chord to which it does not properly *belong*. It is one half-step below a chord tone and, before resolving upward to *join* the chord, adds spice to the static structure.

C6 (Chord Tones)   C6 (with Lower Neighbor)

Lower Neighbor   C6 Chord Tones

In the following composition SIXTH SENSE, all left hand chords are to be played as stop chords (blocked) in root position. Notice the added color of the "lower neighbor". This is one of the tones frequently used in improvisation.

SIXTH SENSE

By MARVIN KAHN

(L.N. = Lower Neighbor)

Western Style Bass

The Added Sixth Chord may be used to produce a Western Style Bass. The formula is *root*, *fifth*, *sixth*, *fifth*. The third of the chord is omitted. The rhythmic pattern is as follows:

This bass is most useful in western style folk songs.

The following song, MY LITTLE BUCKAROO, is to be played with this bass style.

The arrangement is written out to help the student understand the rhythmical problems. The chord symbols appear above each measure. All chords used have been learned in this book, except C♯7. Play this as given.

MY LITTLE BUCKAROO

Words by
JACK SCHOLL

Music by
M. K. JEROME

PART III

FLAT CHORDS

Up to now we have dealt with chords built upon white notes. In the flat (black) key chords, the same interval relationship maintains, of course. Visually, there are three groups.

FIRST GROUP

D♭(C♯), E♭, and A♭ major triads have the same outline. Notice that the spelling of these major triads consists of BLACK-WHITE-BLACK.

Visual Table of Major Triads

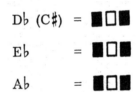

All changes in *quality* use the same formula as for the white note chords. The following table will show the four changes in quality for each of the above chords:

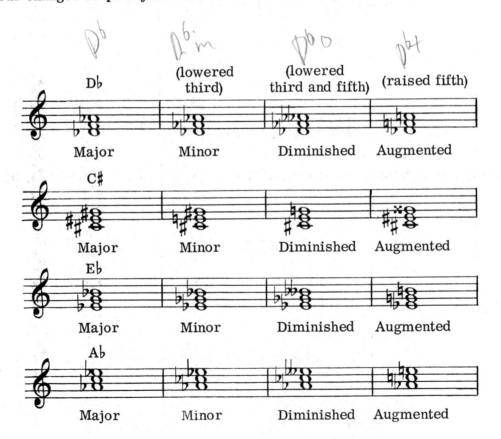

<u>KEYBOARD DRILL</u>:

Play cross-hand arpeggios (runs) for D♭ (C♯), E♭, and A♭ triads for Major, Minor, Diminished, Major, and Augmented *qualities*.

SECOND GROUP

The second group is F♯ (G♭) in which only black keys are used for the Major Triad.

(■■■)

The following are the four changes in *quality* for the F♯ and G♭ chords:

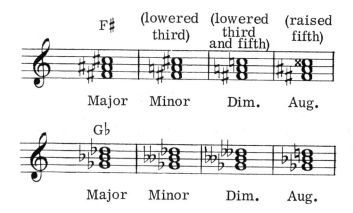

THIRD GROUP

B♭ is the only chord in the third grouping. The Major Triad consists of **BLACK-WHITE-WHITE.**

(■□□)

The following are the four changes in *quality* for the B♭ chord:

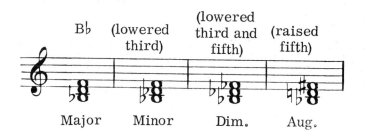

KEYBOARD DRILL:

Play cross-hand arpeggios (runs) for D♭, E♭, A♭, F♯, and B♭ triads in Major, Minor, Diminished, and Augmented *qualities*.

SUMMARY OF FLAT TRIADS

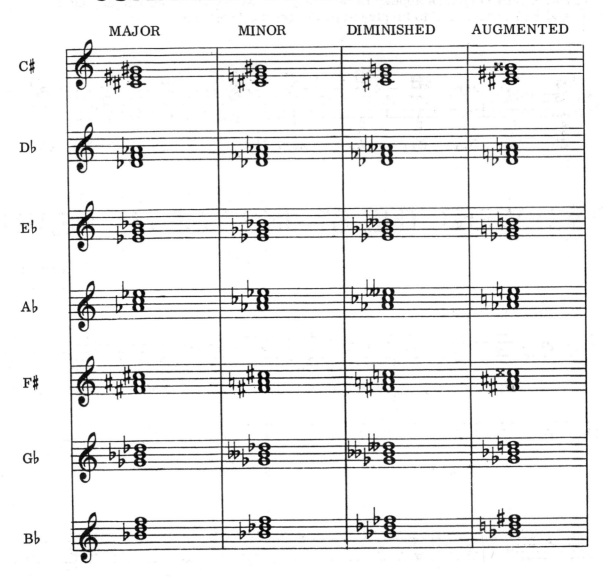

VISUAL SUMMARY OF FLAT TRIADS
(Root Position)

The following song, ZING, WENT THE STRINGS OF MY HEART, uses some of the flat chords. Play the left hand chords as stop chords (block style). The fill-ins and ending are to be played as written.

The following eleven chords appear in this song. Practice them before playing the song. Note that the Bb and Bb7 chords are to be played in the second inversion.

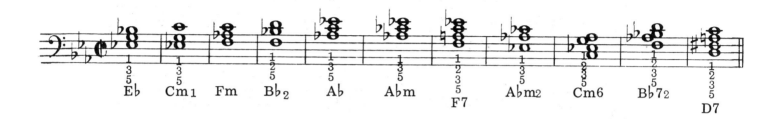

ZING! WENT THE STRINGS OF MY HEART

Words and Music by
JAMES F. HANLEY

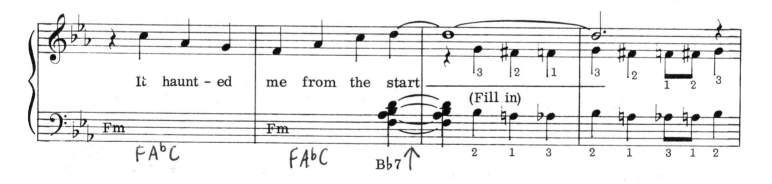

40

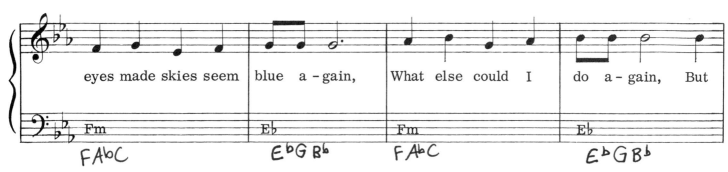

eyes made skies seem | blue a-gain, | What else could I | do a-gain, But

Fm | Eb | Fm | Eb

FAbC | EbGBb | FAbC | EbGBb

keep re-peat-ing through a-gain, "I | love you, | love you!" | I still re-

Cm6   D7 | Eb   F7 | Bb7 | Bb7   Bb+ | Eb

CEbGA   DF#AC | EbGBb   FACEb | FAbBbD | FAbBbD | EbGBb

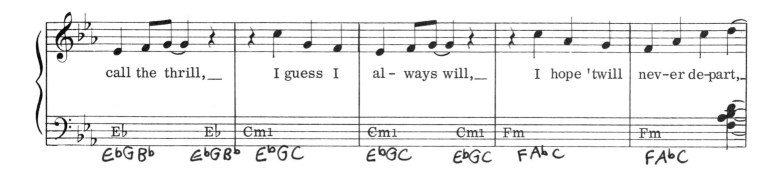

call the thrill,__ | I guess I | al-ways will,__ | I hope 'twill | nev-er de-part,__

Eb | Eb   Cm1 | Cm1 | Cm1   Fm | Fm

EbGBb | EbGBb   EbGC | EbGC | EbGC   FAbC | FAbC

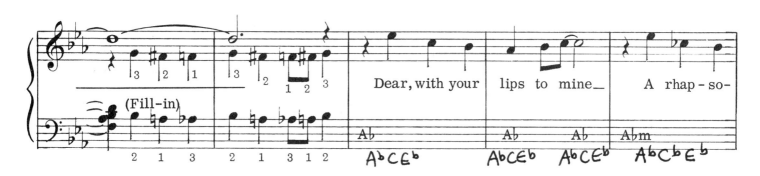

(Fill-in)

Dear, with your | lips to mine__ | A rhap-so-

Ab | Ab   Ab | Abm

AbCEb | AbCEb   AbCEb | AbCbEb

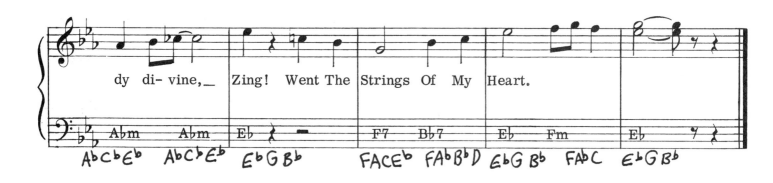

dy di-vine,__ | Zing! Went The | Strings Of My | Heart.

Abm   Abm | Eb | F7   Bb7 | Eb   Fm | Eb

AbCbEb   AbCbEb | EbGBb | FACEb   FAbBbD | EbGBb   FAbC | EbGBb

Summary of Chords 43

Part I

Seventh Chord Structure 45
Dominant Seventh 45
Minor Seventh 45
Seventh Chord Inversions 46
Review of 3/4 Meter Bass Patterns 48
Minor Seventh Flatted Fifth 51
Diminished Seventh 53
Melodic Improvisation 55
Single Note Bass 57
Augmented Seventh 58
Major Seventh 58

Part II

Waltz Bass Patterns (3/4) 61
Waltz Swing Bass 61
Waltz Stop Bass 61
"Broken 5 and 10" 62
Broken tenth and inversion 65
Arpeggiated Bass 65
Inverted Waltz Bass 66

Part III

Fox-trot Bass Patterns (¢) 71
Swing Bass 71
Broken "5 and 10" 71
Broken Fifth and Seventh 73
Broken Swing Bass 76
Doubling Melody 76
Summary of Bass Patterns 78

Songs

All Broken Up 47
Your Eyes Have Told Me So 49
Flatted Fifth Bounce 52
Fine and Dandy 54
Memories 31
Sixth Sense 33
My Little Buckaroo 34
Zing! Went the Strings of My Heart 39

SUMMARY OF CHORDS
TRIADS

In Book I of this course all <u>triads</u> and changes in <u>quality</u> were shown and explored. Also presented were chords of the Added Sixth (both Major and Minor) and the Dominant Seventh. For quick reference there follows a summary of all chords learned up to this point. All are shown in the Root Position, and the proper chord symbol is given under each chord.

SUMMARY OF CHORDS cont'd

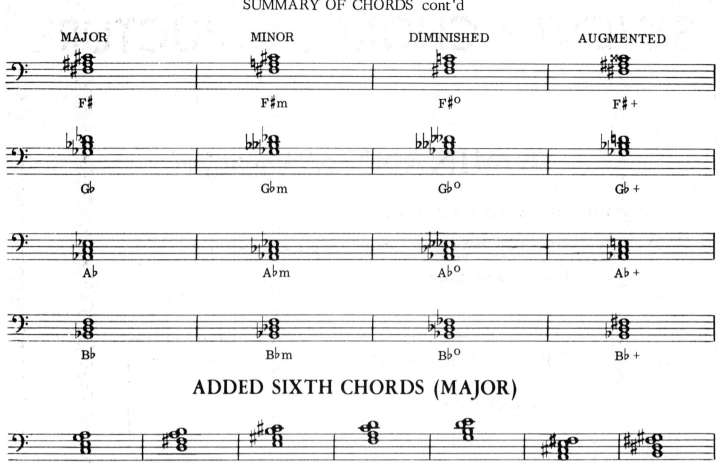

MAJOR	MINOR	DIMINISHED	AUGMENTED
F♯	F♯m	F♯°	F♯+
G♭	G♭m	G♭°	G♭+
A♭	A♭m	A♭°	A♭+
B♭	B♭m	B♭°	B♭+

ADDED SIXTH CHORDS (MAJOR)

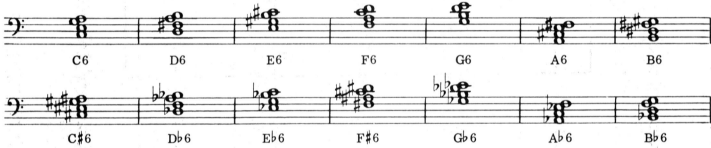

C6 D6 E6 F6 G6 A6 B6

C♯6 D♭6 E♭6 F♯6 G♭6 A♭6 B♭6

ADDED SIXTH CHORDS (MINOR)

Cm6 Dm6 Em6 Fm6 Gm6 Am6 Bm6

C♯m6 D♭m6 E♭m6 F♯m6 G♭m6 A♭m6 B♭m6

DOMINANT SEVENTH CHORDS

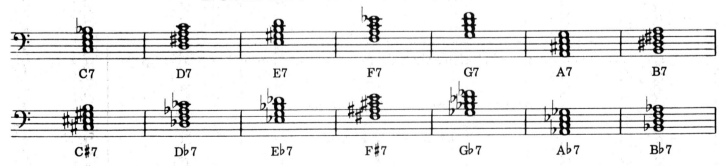

C7 D7 E7 F7 G7 A7 B7

C♯7 D♭7 E♭7 F♯7 G♭7 A♭7 B♭7

SEVENTH CHORDS STRUCTURE

DOMINANT SEVENTH

This chord was introduced in Book I, but to review:

FORMULA = <u>root, third, fifth,</u> <u>seventh</u> (one whole step below the octave)

            Major Triad   Minor Third

> DOMINANT SEVENTH CHORD SYMBOL = Root plus "7"
>
>   Example: C7 = C-E-G-B♭
>
>   D7 = D-F♯-A-C
>
>   etc.

MINOR SEVENTH

This is the second change in <u>quality</u> of a Seventh chord.

FORMULA = Minor Triad plus the Seventh

                      or

      root, <u>lowered</u> third, fifth, seventh

        Minor Triad   Minor Third

> MINOR SEVENTH CHORD SYMBOL = Root plus "m7" or "mi7"
>
>   Example: Cm7 = C-E♭-G-B♭
>
>   Dmi7 = D-F-A-C
>
>   etc.

DRILL: Play cross-hand full block chord for C_7, D_7, E_7, F_7, G_7, A_7 and B_7; then Cm_7, Dm_7, Em_7, Fm_7, Gm_7, Am_7, and Bm_7, as in the following example:

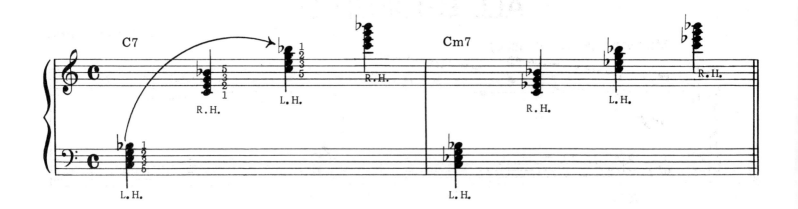

SEVENTH CHORD INVERSIONS

All Seventh chords may be inverted three ways. The following example shows all inversions of C_7 and Cm_7. Practice this drill, hands separately, doing the same for D_7 Dm_7, E_7 Em_7, F_7 Fm_7, G_7 Gm_7, A_7 Am_7, Db_7 Dbm_7 ($C\sharp$), Eb_7 Ebm_7, $F\sharp_7$ $F\sharp m_7$ (Gb), Ab_7 Abm_7 and Bb_7 Bbm_7.

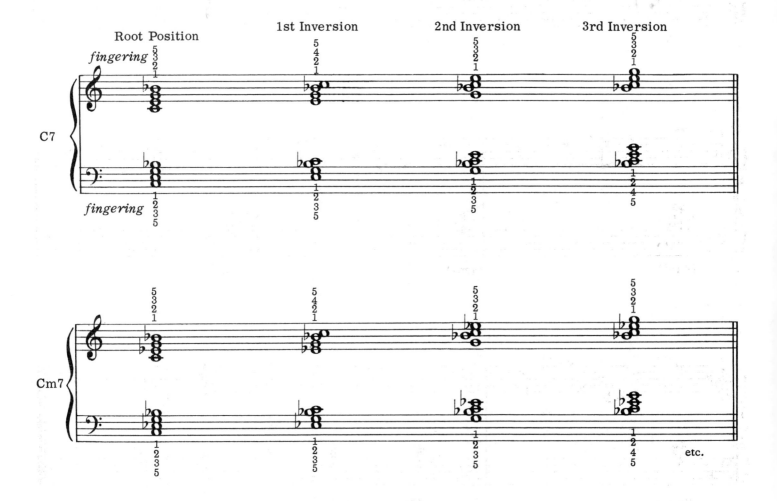

MELODIC INVERSION

The composition ALL BROKEN UP features the right hand in <u>melodic inversions</u> (single notes) of the block chords played by the left hand. This is a very valuable device in developing your improvisational ideas. Notice how effective the <u>melodic inversion</u> is in either direction, spelling <u>up</u> the chord as well as <u>down</u>.

ALL BROKEN UP

By MARVIN KAHN

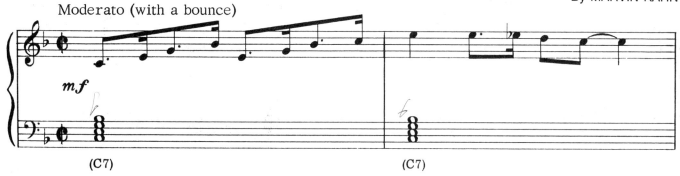

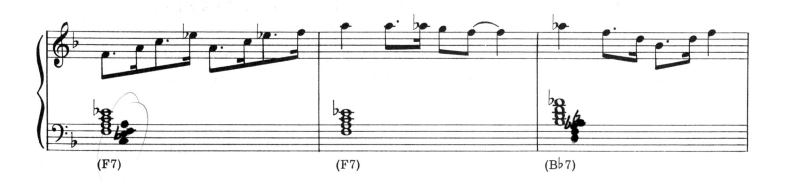

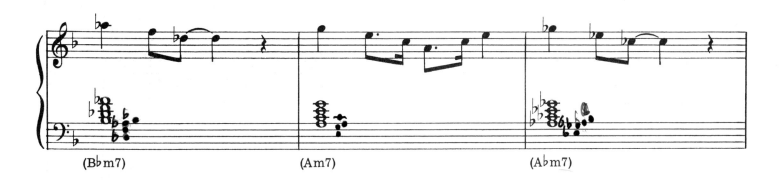

48

Review of 3/4 Meter Bass Patterns

BROKEN CHORD

BLOCK CHORD, DOMINANT SEVENTH

ARPEGGIATED CHORD

"BROKEN 5 and 10" (Open position triads)

BLOCK CHORD, ROOT POSITION

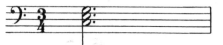

OPEN SEVENTH

root   fifth   seventh

BLOCK CHORD, INVERSIONS

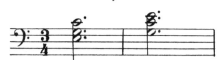

The beautiful waltz, YOUR EYES HAVE TOLD ME SO, utilizes the Added Sixth, Dominant Seventh and Minor Seventh chords. All chords will be played in root position except C7 and Bb which are in the second inversion. Three staves are used as on a regular song sheet. The top staff is the singer's part, and the bottom two are for the piano.

PRACTICE PROCEDURE:

1. The following left hand chords are found in YOUR EYES HAVE TOLD ME SO. Learn them well.

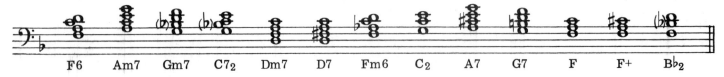

F6   Am7   Gm7   C7₂   Dm7   D7   Fm6   C₂   A7   G7   F   F+   Bb₂

2. Play all left hand chords as <u>stop</u> (block) chords.
3. <u>Play the right hand part an octave higher than written.</u> (This is done to allow a better register for the left hand chords.)
4. Make your own arrangement of this song using the various types of bass patterns just reviewed.

YOUR EYES HAVE TOLD ME SO

Words by
GUS KAHN and EGBERT VAN ALSTYNE

Music by
WALTER BLAUFUSS

50

MINOR SEVENTH FLATTED FIFTH

The next change in <u>quality</u> of a Seventh chord is the Minor Seventh Flatted Fifth. ("Flatted" means lowered one half-step.)

FORMULA = Diminished Triad plus the Seventh

root, lowered third, lowered fifth, seventh

Diminished Triad   Minor Third

The seventh tone is the same as in the Dominant and Minor Sevenths, i.e., one whole step below the octave.

MINOR SEVENTH FLATTED FIFTH CHORD SYMBOL = Root plus "m7-5"

or "m7b5"

Cm7b5

Example: Cm7-5 = C-Eb-Gb-Bb

Dm7b5 = D-F-Ab-C

etc.

DRILL:

Play the following exercises in Seventh chords based on C; then do the same for D, E, F, G, A and B.

Now that we have learned three changes <u>of quality</u> in Seventh chords (Dominant Seventh, Minor Seventh, and Minor Seventh Flatted Fifth), our melodic improvisation can become more interesting musically. In the following composition, FLATTED FIFTH BOUNCE, notice how the right hand is made up of notes <u>taken from the left hand chords.</u> These notes are known as <u>chord tones.</u> The "lower neighbor" tone is also used and is indicated with the symbol "L.N." Before attempting FLATTED FIFTH BOUNCE it is advisable to study and learn the 10 chords which it contains. We show them below.

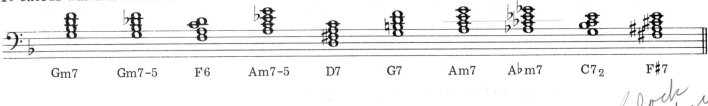

Gm7   Gm7-5   F6   Am7-5   D7   G7   Am7   A♭m7   C7₂   F♯7

FLATTED FIFTH BOUNCE

By MARVIN KAHN

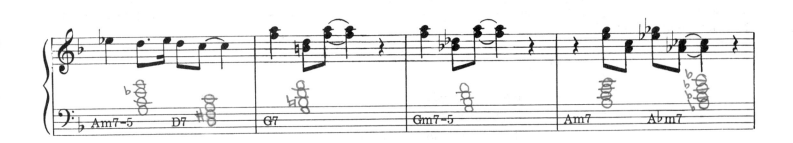

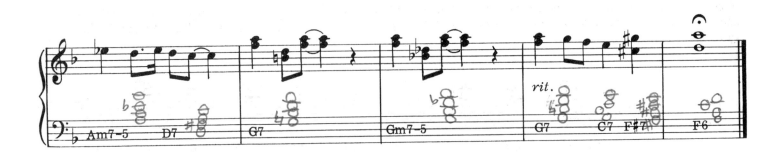

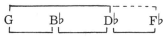

DIMINISHED SEVENTH

The next change in quality is the Diminished Seventh Chord. The chord is now getting smaller in size.

FORMULA = Diminished Triad plus the Seventh, lowered ("diminished") to $1\frac{1}{2}$ steps below the octave

or

Three adjacent Minor Thirds, e.g:

Diminished Triad Seventh (diminished)

G   B♭   D♭   F♭

Minor Thirds

For easier reading Diminished Sevenths usually take enharmonic spellings and are named for the bottom note. In actual sound there are really only three basic Diminished Seventh chords. In the following three groupings all Diminished Sevenths are shown. Notice how all chords within each grouping contain the same chord tones.

Cdim7   E♭dim7   F♯dim7   Adim7   C♯dim7   Edim7   Gdim7   B♭dim7   Ddim7   Fdim7   G♯dim7   Bdim7

Most publishers of popular songs do not use the Diminished Seventh chord symbol. They usually use the symbol for a Diminished Triad. However, in all cases play a Diminished Seventh, as the Diminished Triad has an incomplete sound.

DIMINISHED CHORD SYMBOL = Root plus "o" or "dim"

Example: G° (Gdim) = G-B♭-D♭

But always think of this as

DIMINISHED SEVENTH CHORD SYMBOL = Root plus "dim7"

Example: Gdim7 = G-B♭-D♭-F♭

or, enharmonically = G-B♭-C♯-E

The Diminished Seventh is used in the following song, FINE AND DANDY. This is a bright show tune and should be played alla breve (cut time). Consider the meter as ¢. Use all chords block style (stop chords). First practice the chords used in this song as given below. The C7 and Cm7 are used in the second inversion; all other chords are in root position. The ending is written out. Play the right hand an octave higher than written.

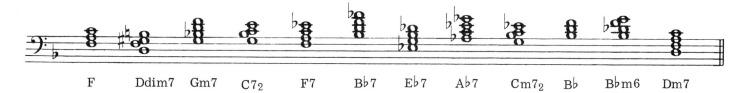

F   Ddim7   Gm7   C7₂   F7   B♭7   E♭7   A♭7   Cm7₂   B♭   B♭m6   Dm7

FINE AND DANDY

Words by
PAUL JAMES

Music by
KAY SWIFT

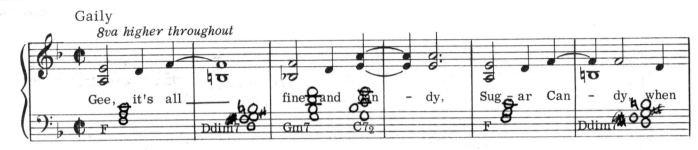

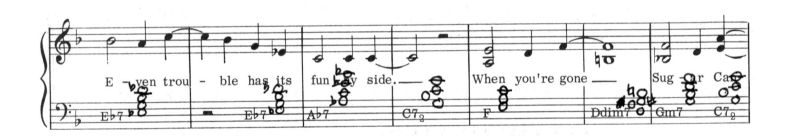

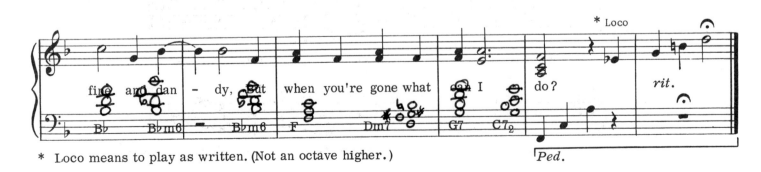

* Loco means to play as written. (Not an octave higher.)

In the next composition, KIND-A-MOODY, try your skill at playing Diminished Sevenths plus some of the other Sevenths you have learned thus far. In the left hand play all block (stop) chords.

KIND-A-MOODY

By MARVIN KAHN

MELODIC IMPROVISATION

The ability to "make up" or invent melodic patterns based on the chordal background of a new song is the mark of the professional jazz pianist. Such fine musicians as Peter Nero, Andre Previn, George Shearing, and Errol Garner, to mention a few, are masters of this art. This amounts to more than mere "musical noodling." It is based on a complete understanding of chords, and a plan of procedure is very important.

1.   We have already learned to break up chords and their inversions into chord tones,
       using them to create passages of melodic and rhythmic interest.

Examples:

CHORD TONES, INVERSIONS

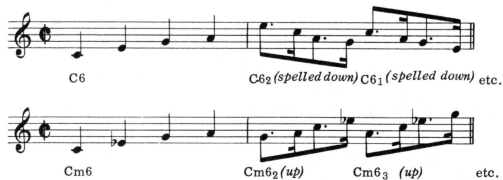

2. We also learned about "lower neighbors." These are tones which are <u>one half step</u> below the chord tone. Lower neighbors add spice to the academic sound of plain chord tones.

Now invent your own melodic patterns for the following chord progressions. Try to use lower neighbors and inverted spellings, both up and down.

MY OWN IMPROVISATION

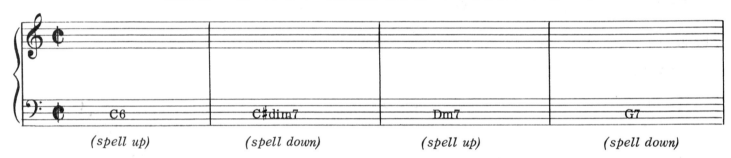

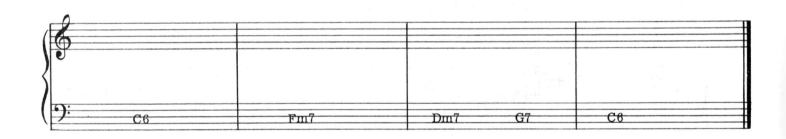

DRILL:

Write in the lower neighbors for the following notes:

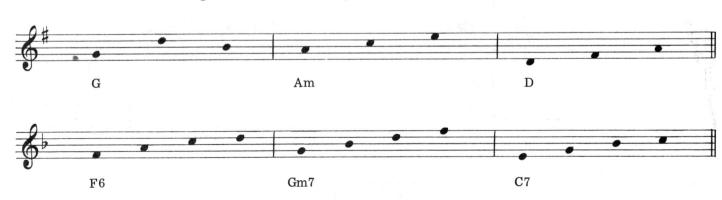

3. Each chord tone has an "upper neighbor" also. The upper neighbor is the <u>next scale tone above</u> the given chord tone. It may be a half or whole step, depending on the key signature. The abbreviation for upper neighbor is "U. N."

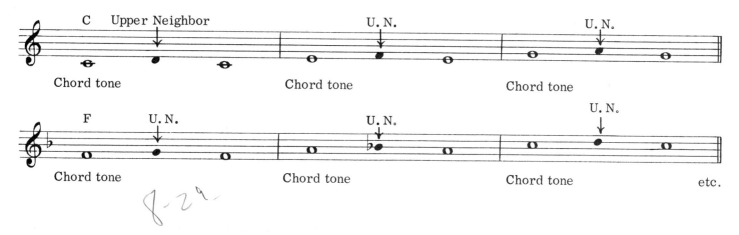

SINGLE NOTE BASS

A single note in the left hand may be used to represent the chord needed in the right hand. It is always a chord tone.

The following composition, BUSY NEIGHBORS, consists of single notes in the left hand, while the melody itself is comprised of chord tones and neighbors, both upper and lower.

ANALYZE this and indicate all neighbors, using the following abbreviations:

L. N. = lower neighbor

U. N. = upper neighbor

C. T. = chord tone

BUSY NEIGHBORS

By MARVIN KAHN

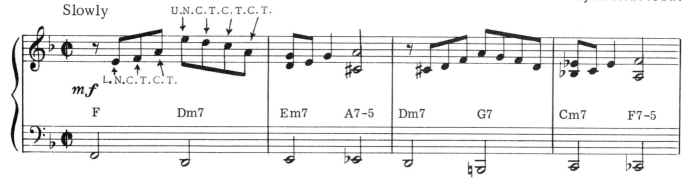

AUGMENTED SEVENTH

FORMULA = Augmented Triad plus the Seventh (one whole step below the octave)

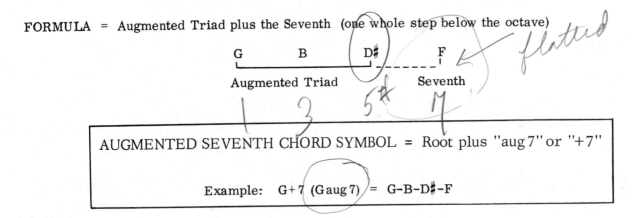

┌───┐
│ AUGMENTED SEVENTH CHORD SYMBOL = Root plus "aug 7" or "+7"   │
│   │
│   Example: G+7 (G aug 7) = G-B-D♯-F   │
└───┘

MAJOR SEVENTH

The last type of Seventh chord is the Major, so called because the interval between the root and the seventh is a <u>major seventh,</u> which is only a half-step below the octave.

FORMULA = Major Triad plus a Major Third

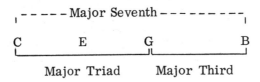

┌───┐
│ MAJOR SEVENTH CHORD SYMBOL = Root plus "maj 7"   │
│   │
│   Example: Fmaj 7 = F-A-C-E   │
└───┘

The Major Seventh chord is used as a replacement for a plain Major Triad in progressive jazz. It has a warm sound, and its many uses will be shown as we progress.

Now let us incorporate the Major Seventh into THE JAPANESE SANDMAN. In this wonderful standard play all chords block style. The right hand is intended for the register as written, not an octave higher. Play the first chord Fmaj7 in this register:

Fmaj7

Note the use of the word <u>tacet.</u> This means silence, do not play. Practice the following chords <u>before</u> playing the song:

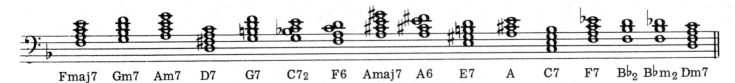

Fmaj7 Gm7 Am7 D7 G7 C7₂ F6 Amaj7 A6 E7 A C7 F7 B♭₂ B♭m₂ Dm7

THE JAPANESE SANDMAN

Words by
RAYMOND B. EGAN

Music by
RICHARD A. WHITING

* TACET means silence

60

WALTZ BASS PATTERNS $\left(\dfrac{3}{4}\right)$

In Book I the Triad was used as the basis of simple left hand bass patterns. Now, with your added knowledge of Sixth and Seventh chords and their inversions, the left hand patterns can now be extended. Let us turn to the Waltz, or $\dfrac{3}{4}$ meter.

WALTZ SWING BASS

FORMULA = First Beat.............single bass note (usually the root of the chord)
Second Beat.............chord
Third Beat.............chord

Thus, if the measure is a G7 chord:

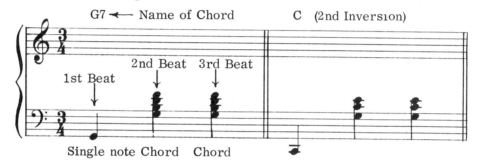

The lowest note of the second beat chord should be a <u>minimum of an octave above the single bass note of the first beat.</u> This produces more of a sweep on the keyboard and adds variety to the tonal range.

<u>TECHNIQUE:</u>

To produce a lilting Waltz Bass, the accent should be on the first beat. <u>Brush</u> the chord, using a gentle stroke on the second and third beats (sometimes called "afterbeats").

WALTZ STOP BASS

This is a variation of the Waltz Swing Bass and is used to avoid the monotony of an "um-chum-chum" sound in the left hand.

FORMULA = First Beat.............single note
Second and Third Beat.............half-note chord, or chord and quarter rest

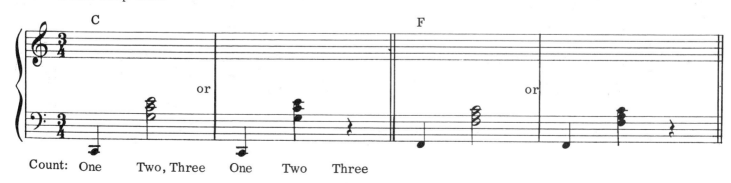

NOTE: The Waltz Stop Bass is most effective when the melody has movement. The following rhythms in the right hand work beautifully with this bass:

However, a 𝅗𝅥. is **not** good with this type bass. (Try it and see for yourself.)

"BROKEN 5 AND 10"

This was explored in Book I and is a welcome addition to the two types of waltz bass mentioned above.

FORMULA (Triad) = First Beat............root

Second Beat..........fifth

Third Beat...........tenth (third)

FORMULA (Seventh Chord) = First Beat............root

Second Beat..........fifth

Third Beat...........seventh

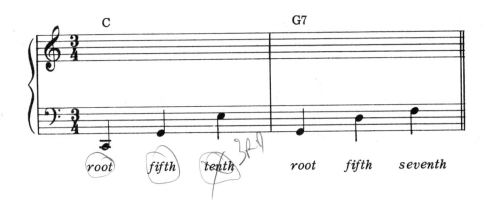

Now let us use all three types of Waltz Bass in the song FOR YOU. The bass patterns form an arrangement. Play this as given, and then try experimenting with a second chorus using your own ideas. The right hand part should be played as written, not an octave higher. Section [B] is all "Broken 5 and 10" Bass. The following chords are used in FOR YOU. Practice them before playing the song.

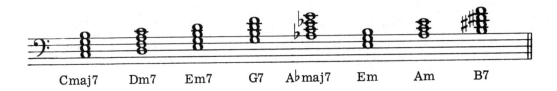

Cmaj7   Dm7   Em7   G7   A♭maj7   Em   Am   B7

FOR YOU

Words by
AL DUBIN

Music by
JOE BURKE

Moderato

I will gath-er stars out of the blue _____ for you, _____ for you. _____ I'll make a string of pearls out of the dew _____ for you, _____ for

BROKEN TENTH AND INVERSION

This is much the same as the "Broken 5 and 10" Bass, except that the first two notes are eighth notes, followed by a quarter note, then an inversion of the chord. The movement created by this rhythm makes an interesting bass pattern.

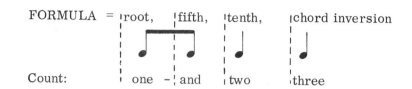

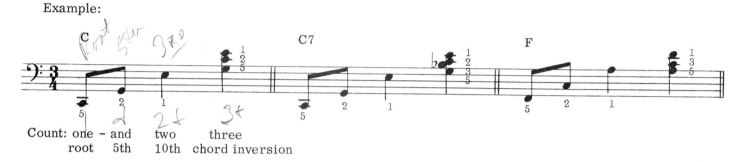

ARPEGGIATED BASS

The Arpeggiated Bass creates movement and is most effective when there is a wait in the melody.

Examples:

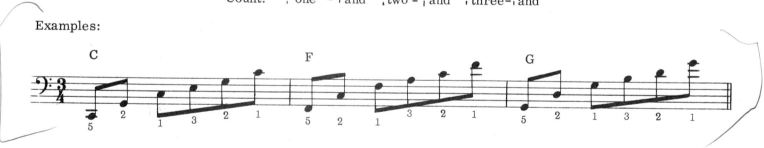

An important rule to remember in playing this type of bass is to play the root, then skip to the fifth, omitting the <u>third</u> until it occurs further on up the keyboard as a <u>tenth.</u> This avoids a muddy sound.

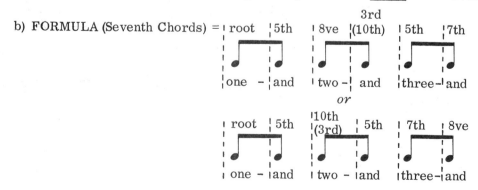

Examples:

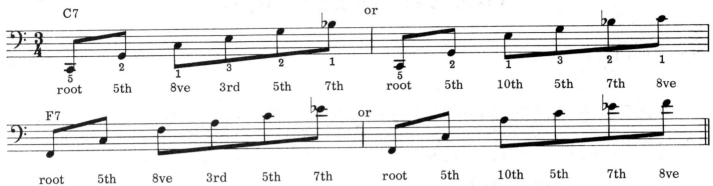

INVERTED WALTZ BASS

By changing the position of a left hand chord (inversion) on the third beat, a new color is added to the left hand pattern.

FORMULA = | First Beat | Second Beat | Third Beat
| single bass note | chord | chord in different position

Examples:

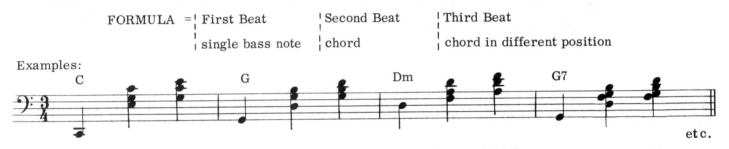

Now, all these bass patterns will be put to use in the beautiful standard Waltz, **TILL WE MEET AGAIN.** The first 8 measures are written out, and the bass patterns are named in each bar. For the remainder of the song (24 measures) only the names appear. You are to play whatever is indicated. When you have mastered this, try using your own ideas based on the bass patterns you have learned thus far. And remember, <u>there is no set way to play a popular song.</u> The proficient "pop" pianist rarely plays a tune the same way twice.

The following abbreviations are used along with the chord symbols:

BR. 10 INV.	=	Broken 10th and Inversion
INV.	=	Inverted Waltz Bass
ARP.	=	Arpeggiated Bass
W. STOP	=	Waltz Stop Bass
BR. 5 & 10	=	"Broken 5 and 10"
STOP	=	Block Chord

NOTE: This arrangement avoids using the Waltz Swing Bass. The more this sound can be eliminated, the better. It is the mark of the beginner and tends to become boring. Also, remember that the harmonization (chord structure) called for by the chord symbol is meant to continue until another chord symbol occurs.

TILL WE MEET AGAIN

Words by
RAYMOND B. EGAN

Music by
RICHARD A. WHITING

In the following lilting waltz, FASCINATION, the entire arrangement is written out. Ananlyze the bass patterns and observe the movement created by an Arpeggiated Bass where the melody has a wait, as in measure
10, 12, etc. Play this as given, then try arranging this song using your own ideas. Play the right hand an
octave higher than written.

FASCINATION

Words by
JEAN REYNOLDS DAVIS

Music by
F. D. MARCHETTI

FOX-TROT BASS PATTERNS (₵)

SWING BASS

The Swing Bass is a basic pattern used in the ₵ ($\frac{2}{2}$) meter. It is a "necessary evil," and as we progress, more ways will be shown to eliminate it. It was first introduced in RAGTIME and DIXIELAND styles.

FORMULA = First Beat.........single bass note (usually the root of the chord)

Second Beat........chord

Third Beat.........single bass note (usually the root of the chord)

Fourth Beat........chord

STOP CHORD

This means to play the chord block style and hold for the length of time indicated.

The Stop Chord is a welcome relief as a bass pattern. Most "fill-ins" in the right hand sound especially effective if the left hand chord is sustained (stop chord).

"BROKEN 5 AND 10"

FORMULA = root, 5th, 10th (back to) 5th

This bass (abbreviated "Br. 5 & 10") can be used in quarter notes (one to a beat), eighth notes (two to a beat), or dotted eighth and sixteenths as shown below.

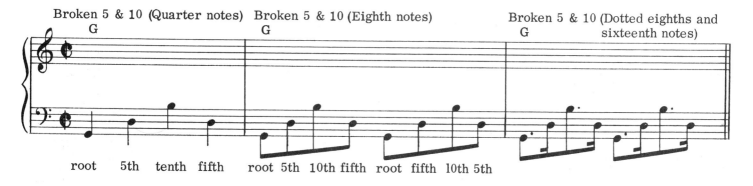

These three bass patterns are now used together in the well known standard, PRETTY BABY. Play the arrangement as given, then try one of your own. The right hand should be an octave higher than written. The first 4 measures are written out in full.

PRETTY BABY

Words by
GUS KAHN

Music by
TONY JACKSON and EGBERT VAN ALSTYNE

BROKEN FIFTH AND SEVENTH

FORMULA = root, 5th, 7th (back to) 5th

This bass is used to accommodate a Seventh Chord, and it is the same pattern as the "Broken 5 & 10," the only change being that the <u>seventh</u> of the chord is used as the third note instead of the <u>tenth.</u>

Examples:

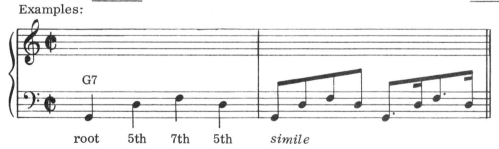

Now, using the four bass patterns learned thus far, let us incorporate them into an arrangement of the beautiful standard, TOO MARVELOUS FOR WORDS. The Swing Bass is avoided as before. The arrangement is written out and the bass patterns abbreviated. Analyze the patterns, then play the song again changing the given patterns to work out your own arrangement. Play the right hand as it is written and not an octave higher.

Note the use of the Arpeggiated Bass on the Dm7 chord in measures 17 and 18. This is the same pattern learned for the $\frac{3}{4}$ meter. Also analyze the "fill-ins" in measures 21 and 22. You will see that the left hand is merely spelling the chord down, creating an interesting sound. This is an easy and effective "fill-in" device.

TOO MARVELOUS FOR WORDS

Words by
JOHNNY MERCER

Music by
RICHARD A. WHITING

BROKEN SWING BASS

This is a most useful pattern and adds more movement than the Swing Bass. It consists of the chord being broken into two units.

Examples:

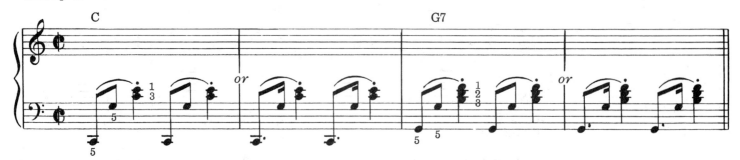

NOTE: The Broken Swing Bass is most effective when the rhythm of the melody is in a 𝅗𝅥 or 𝅘𝅥. 𝅘𝅥𝅮 rhythm.

DOUBLING MELODY

This is a pleasing device which often occurs in "pick-up" measures. It consists of playing the same melody notes in each hand, preferably two octaves apart.

Try the Broken Swing Bass in the song APRIL SHOWERS. It will add interest and movement to the half notes in the melody, as in measure 1, etc. The first part of the arrangement is written out. After that you're on your own. Play the right hand an octave higher than written, except where it is marked "LOCO". The ending and "fill-ins" are also written out. Note the use of single bass notes in measures 13 through 16. These notes are taken from the chord indicated by the chord symbol. The use of single notes is very effective, as it relieves the "chordy" sound, particularly where four chord changes are indicated for one measure as in measure 15.

If you analyze the "fill-in" in measure 3, you will see that it is merely the Gmaj7 spelled down. In measure 7, where this occurs again, the Gmaj7 is spelled up. This change of direction produces an interesting variation in the melodic line.

APRIL SHOWERS

Words by
B. G. DeSYLVA

Music by
LOUIS SILVERS

SUMMARY OF BASS PATTERNS
Waltz

At this point we would do well to summarize what we have learned thus far about bass patterns in Waltz and Fox-trot rhythms. The following chart is presented for your convenience and reference.

9. INVERTED WALTZ BASS — Abbr. = Inv.

Fox-Trot

1. SWING BASS — Abbr. = Sw.

2. STOP CHORD — Abbr. = Stop

3. BROKEN FIFTH AND TENTH — Abbr. = Br. 5 & 10

4. BROKEN FIFTH AND SEVENTH — Abbr. = Br. 5 & 7

5. BROKEN SWING BASS — Abbr. = Br. Sw.

AUTUMN IN NEW YORK is considered one of the great all time standards. This entire arrangement, including an introduction, is written out with every chord symbol and bass pattern abbreviation indicated above the singer's part. There is nothing in this arrangement that has not been presented in this book. Play it liltingly and freely, and listen to yourself so that you can produce a singing tone.

AUTUMN IN NEW YORK

Words and Music by
VERNON DUKE

© 1934 (Renewed) WARNER BROS. INC.

Summary of Chords 83
9th Chords 85
Dominant 9th Chords 85
How to Use 9th Chords In the Left Hand 85
9th Chords and The Swing Bass 86
The 9th As a Substitute Chord 89
Other Types of 9th Chords 90
Harmony For the Right Hand 92
How To Use 9th's In the Right Hand 92
Passing Tones 95
The Dominant 7th Chord With a Flatted 9th 102
The Dominant 7th With a Flatted 9th As a Substitute Chord 103
The Use of the Flatted 5th and Raised 5th in Combination With 9th 105
The Suspended 4th Chord 106
The Dominant 7th Chord With Suspended 4th 106
The Dominant 9th Chord With Suspended 4th 106
Best Voicings of the Dominant 9th Chord With Suspended 4th 106
11th Chords 109
Major 11th Chords 109
Dominant 11th Chords 110
Augmented 11th Chords 110
Minor 11th Chords 110
13th Chords 111
Dominant 13th Chords 111
Augmented 11th, Added 13th Chords 111
Bitonality 112
The Pedal Point 113
Working From a Lead Sheet 119

Songs

It Had To Be You 87
Blues On the March 89
Slow and Easy 91
Melody With Ninths 94
The Birth of the Blues 96
What's New? 99
Mirage 104
Days of Wine and Roses 107
A Time For Love 114
Body and Soul 117
April In Paris 119

In Book II of this series entitled "Guidelines to Improvisation" all chords up to the formation of the Major 7th were discussed. By way of review the following table is presented which can also serve as a reference chart for this book.

Summary of Chords

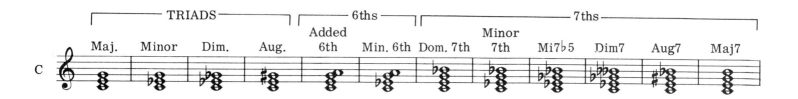

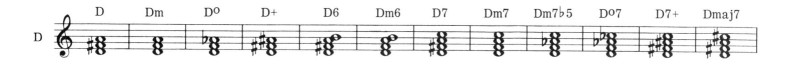

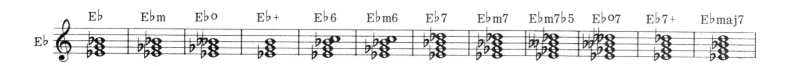

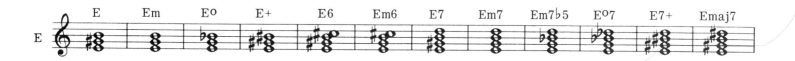

Editors note: The following enharmonic chords have been omitted but can easily be found in the above chart. For C♯ chords see D♭; for G♭ chords see F♯; for C♭ chords see B.

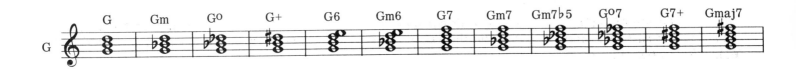

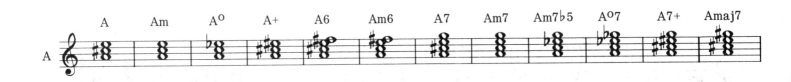

Editor's note: *Certain abbreviations used in popular sheet music are synonymous and are freely interchanged. Examples: 7+ and 7+5 or ♯5, -5 and ♭5, °7 and dim 7, -9 and ♭9.*

9th Chords

At this point of study we will extend our chord knowledge to include the 9th of the chord. An easy way to find this interval is to realize that it has the same name as the 2nd degree of the scale, but is nine steps from the root. Thus the 9th of C is D.(D is also the 2nd degree of the scale.) Write out and play this drill on 9th's:

ROOT	9th		ROOT	9th
C	D ⎱		F♯.	
D♭.	E♭ ⎰ Examples		G	
D			A♭.	
E♭.			A	
E			B♭.	
F			B	

The 9th of the chord creates a dissonance or tension that is a welcome sound in harmony. The first 9th chord to be discussed will be the Dominant 9th chord. The symbol is the root followed by 9 e. g. C9 = C (dominant) 9th.

Dominant 9th Chords

(Symbol: 9)

FORMULA = Dominant 7th chord plus major 3rd.

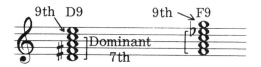

How to Use 9th Chords in the Left Hand

Inasmuch as dominant 9th chords have five tones, it is rather awkward to play the full chord in one hand. Therefore, eliminate one of the tones, namely the root. Thus when playing a G9 chord, the left hand plays only BDFA:

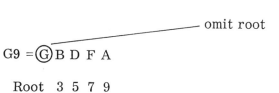

——————————— omit root

G9 = ⓖ B D F A

Root 3 5 7 9

NOTE: On song sheets 9th chords are not too common. They are usually indicated in lush or harmonically advanced songs.

9th Chords and the Swing Bass

The swing bass can use a 9th chord formation by playing the root on the 1st and 3rd beats and the full 9th chord (3-5-7-9) on the 2nd and 4th beats.

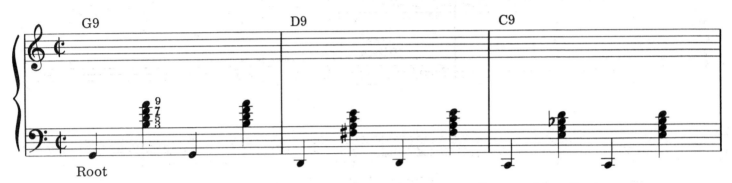

The following great standard "It Had To Be You" uses this effect.

Practice the following left hand chords found in this song:

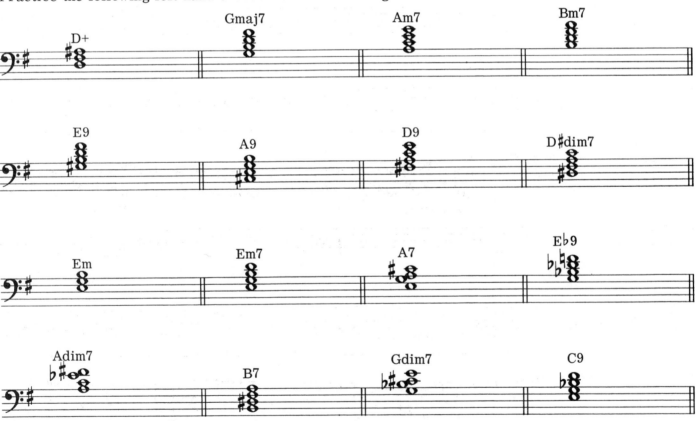

IT HAD TO BE YOU

Words by
GUS KAHN

Music by
ISHAM JONES

The 9th as a Substitute Chord

Even when not called for on the sheet music, a 9th chord may often be substituted for a 7th chord. For example, if the indicated chord is C7, a C9 may be played instead.

This device of using substitute chords is one of the most common used by modern players to "dress up" old songs.

The following musical example – "Blues on the March" – first shows a harmonization using dominant 7th chords. Then the same melody is harmonized with dominant 9th chords.

Listen to the difference in tone color:

BLUES ON THE MARCH

(USING 7th CHORDS)

By MARVIN KAHN

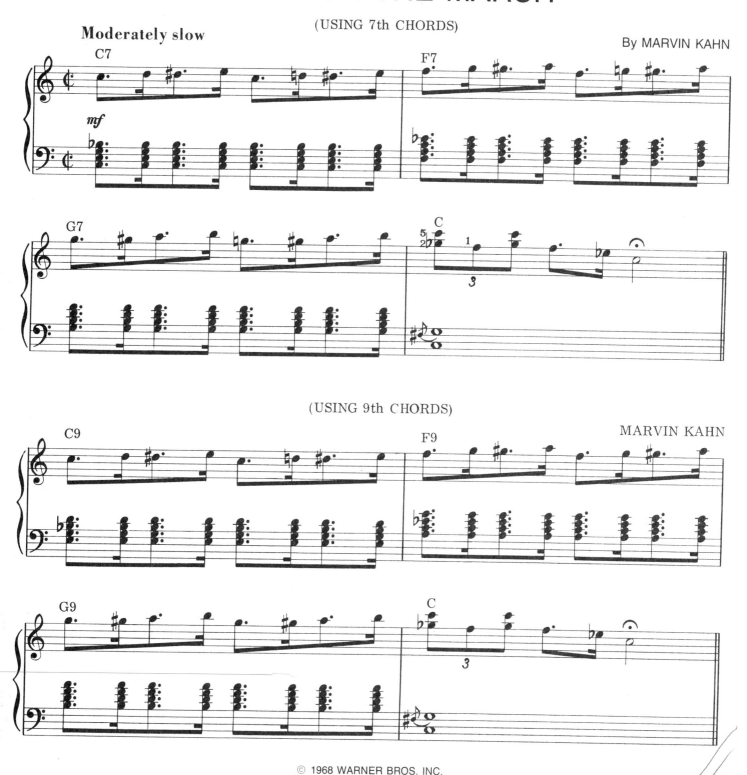

(USING 9th CHORDS)

MARVIN KAHN

Other Types of 9th Chords

THE MINOR 9th (symbol: m9 or mi9) = minor 7th with an added 9th.

Example: Cm7 = C E♭ G B♭, Cm9 = C E♭ G B♭ D

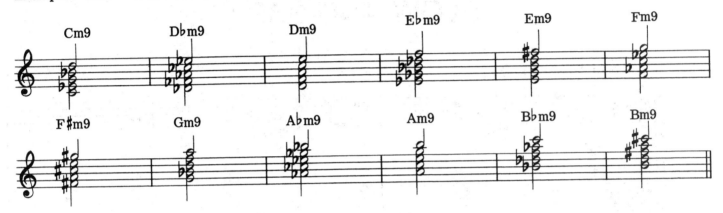

THE MAJOR 9th (symbol: maj9) = major 7th with an added 9th.

Example: Cmaj7 = C E G B, Cmaj9 = C E G B D

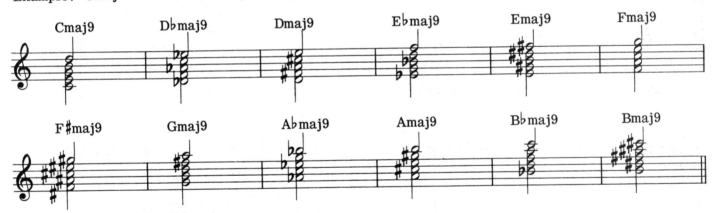

THE AUGMENTED 9th (symbol: 9+) = augmented 7th with an added 9th.

Example: C7+ = C E G♯ B♭, C9+ = C E G♯ B♭ D

To reinforce the sound of the left hand 9th chord play the following composition in the manner suggested by the title. The hidden dissonance of the 9th adds a subtle spice to the harmonization.

Also notice the use of the Fmaj7 chord rather than an F or F6 chord. In modern playing, as we learned in Book II, the major seventh is often substituted for the plain major triad or the triad with an added 6; this too creates a welcome dissonance.

SLOW AND EASY

By MARVIN KAHN

Harmony for the Right Hand

So far, the right hand melody has been played mostly in single notes. A fuller, richer sound will result, however, if one or more notes are added below the single melody note.

All melody notes may be harmonized using any or all of the tones found in the left hand chord. Thus, if the melody note is C, and the chord is C7:

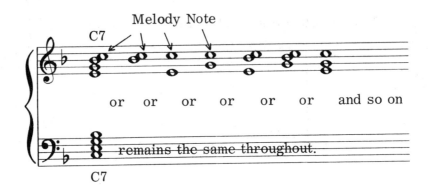

How to Use 9th's in the Right Hand

The 9th of any given chord can be used as part of the harmonization of the melody in the right hand. Its use is highly recommended to add color to an otherwise ordinary harmonization.

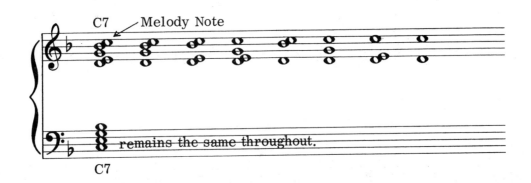

Each player will have to determine which of the above versions of the right hand harmonizations is appropriate to the song being played and which is most pleasing to his ear.

NOTE: An easy way to include the 9th of a given chord as part of the right hand harmonization is to make it the <u>first</u> note to be added beneath the given melody note. Then other tones may be added.

Drill on Dominant 9th's

Example:

Add 9th's below each of these melody notes. . . .

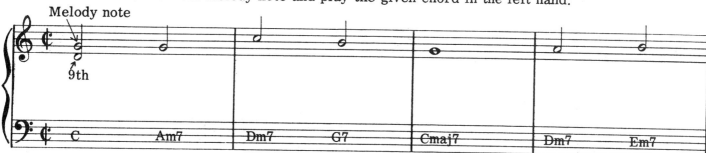

DRILL using m9th's, maj9th's, and 9+'s as well as dominant 9th's.

Add the 9th below the melody note and play the given chord in the left hand.

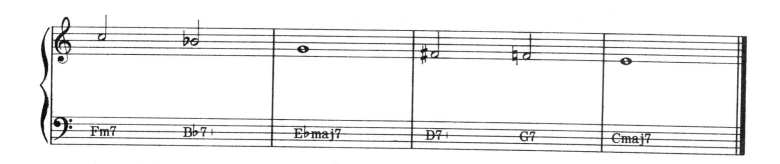

The following composition "Melody With Ninths" illustrates the use of the 9th in the right hand harmonization. Notice that the <u>left hand</u> chords are indicated as 9th's because of that note appearing in the <u>right hand</u> harmonization. This will often appear on sheet music in the same way. Listen to the added richness in sound:

MELODY WITH NINTHS

By MARVIN KAHN

Half Steps and Whole Steps

A half step is the distance from one key to the next regardless of color.

EXAMPLES OF HALF STEPS

A whole step is the distance from one key to the second key away regardless of color.

EXAMPLES OF WHOLE STEPS

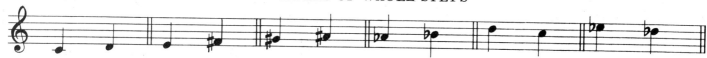

Passing Tones

A passing tone connects chord tones by step. Passing tones are used to give added flexibility and interest to right hand improvisations. Below you will find examples of different types of passing tones. (For the sake of simplicity, all examples are based on a C major triad.) The abbreviation P. T. will be used to indicate passing tones.

C. T. = chord tone, L. N. = lower neighbor, U. N. = upper neighbor.

Example 1: PASSING TONES WHICH APPEAR IN THE KEY OF THE PASSAGE:
(called diatonic passing tones)

Example 2: PASSING TONES WHICH CONNECT CHORD TONES BY HALF STEPS
regardless of the key of the passage:
(called chromatic passing tones)

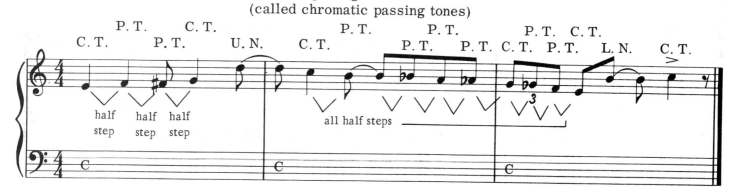

These two types of passing tones can be freely mixed, however.

"The Birth of the Blues" utilizes the substitute 9th chord in the left hand as well as many other chord progressions used in modern music. The left hand is written out completely so that reference and analysis of the printed chord and its chord symbol may be made.

An improvisation in the right hand is given in measures 10 - 16 and 26 - 31. The improvisation is derived from the chordal background plus passing tones, lower and upper neighbors, as well as varied rhythmic patterns.

THE BIRTH OF THE BLUES

Words by
B. G. DeSYLVA and LEW BROWN

Music by
RAY HENDERSON

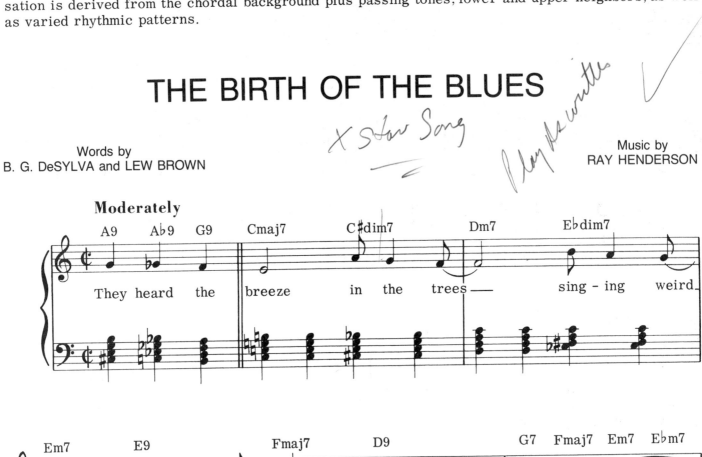

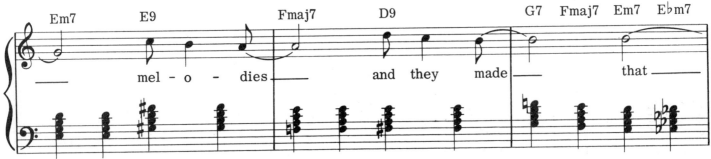

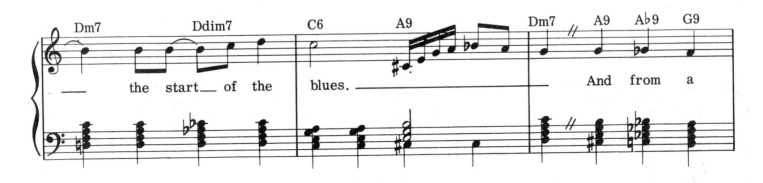

Editor's note: *The expression (inv) means that the root of a chord is not the lowest note.*

98

One of the all time great standards, "What's New?" is presented here in a partial arrangement. It illustrates the use of 9th's in the right hand harmonization as well as in the bass part. In several measures the 9th in the right hand actually is used as part of a passing tone progression, but is emphasized by being played on the accented first beat of the measure to create a deliberate dissonance.

WHAT'S NEW?

Words by
JOHNNY BURKE

Music by
BOB HAGGART

The Dominant 7th Chord with a Flatted 9th

(Symbol: 7-9)

FORMULA = DOMINANT 7th, PLUS MINOR 3rd

In the same manner that we added a 9th to a dominant 7th chord in order to form a dominant 9th chord, we can add a 9th which has been lowered a half step in order to form a dominant 7th chord with a flatted 9th. For example, C9 consists of the notes C E G Bb D. C7-9 consists of the notes C E G Bb Db.

Study and play the following table of chords. It shows the spelling of all the dominant 7th chords with a flatted 9th.

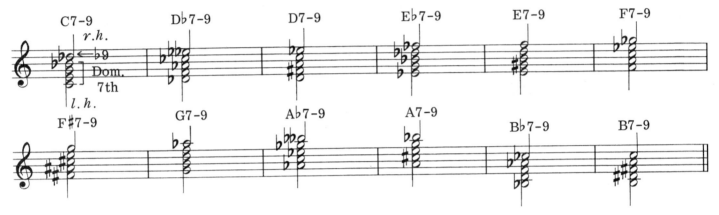

Dominant sevenths with flatted 9ths may be used as:

1. part of the right hand harmonization

2. part of the left hand chord.

In the following drill write in the flatted 9th under the given melody note. To develop the technique of harmonizing a melody using a flatted 9th, make this the first tone in your harmonization.

Example: G7-9

Left hand plays dominant 7th.

When the sound of the flatted 9th is desired in the left hand, the root may be omitted to make the fingering easier. This was the same procedure followed with the dominant 9th chord. (See p. 6.)

The Dominant 7th with a Flatted 9th as a Substitute Chord

As in the case of the dominant 9th chord, the dominant 7th with a flatted 9th may be substituted for the ordinary dominant 7th chord. Thus, if the indicated chord in the sheet music is C7, a C7-9 may be played instead.

Drill: Rewrite the following 7th chords as 7-9 chords:

Example:

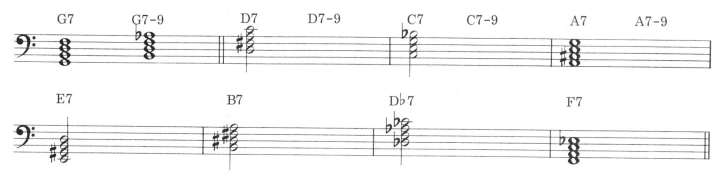

QUESTION: Which chord should be substituted for C7—C9 or C7-9 ?
ANSWER: If the note D (the 9th of C) appears in the melody use C9...

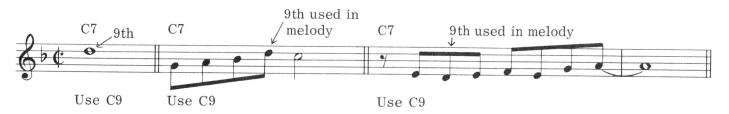

If the note D♭ (the flatted 9th of C) appears in the melody use C7-9,...

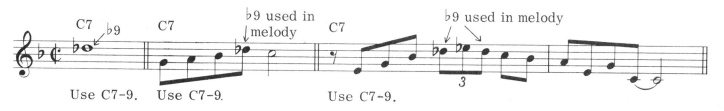

If neither D nor D♭ appear in the melody, either C9 or C7-9 may be used...

Cases in which the 9th does not appear in the melody can be made more interesting by stringing together different substitutes for the basic chord. For example, use C9 in the first measure of the above example; use C7-9 in the second measure and plain C7 in the third. Or, start with plain C7, change to C7-9 in the second measure and C9 in the third. This device is particularly effective when one chord is repeated for an extended period of time.

The following composition "Mirage" utilizes flatted 9th's as part of the right hand harmony as well as the full substitute left hand chord with the flatted 9th. Listen to the color created by this welcome dissonance. All 9ths and flatted 9ths are marked for analysis.

MIRAGE

By MARVIN KAHN

The Use of the Flatted 5th (-5) and the Raised 5th (+ or +5) in Combination with 9th's

Still more substitutes for the dominant 7th chord may be arrived at by lowering or raising the 5th in combination with the natural or flatted 9th. This gives us a total of six chords which may be substituted for the dominant 7th.

For example, if the chord called for is C7, the following chords can be substituted:

C9 (natural 5, natural 9)   C7-9 (natural 5, flatted 9)

C9-5 (flatted 5, natural 9) $C7^{-5}_{-9}$ (flatted 5, flatted 9)

C9+5 (raised 5, natural 9) $C7^{+5}_{-9}$ (raised 5, flatted 9)

Drill: Write out the six substitute chords for C7, D7, E7, F7 and B♭7.

* * * * * * * * * * * * * * *

Cautionary note: Be sure that the substitute chord does not contain a tone which contradicts a melody note:

For example:

When the melody   When the melody   When the melody
contains the   contains the   contains the
raised 5th   natural 5th   flatted 5th

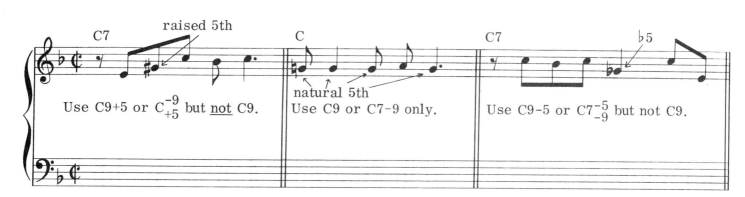

Use C9+5 or C^{-9}_{+5} but not C9.   Use C9 or C7-9 only.   Use C9-5 or $C7^{-5}_{-9}$ but not C9.

In similar fashion avoid using the natural 9th in one hand against a flatted 9th in the other. Thus, the following melody which uses both the raised 5th and the flatted 9th, forces the use of the substitute chord $C7^{+5}_{-9}$.

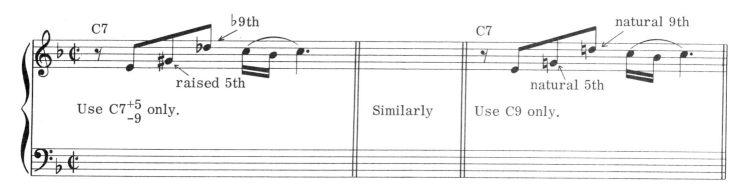

Use $C7^{+5}_{-9}$ only.   Similarly   Use C9 only.

The Suspended 4th Chord

The 4th may replace the 3rd in any dominant 7th or dominant 9th chord. This common device gives us still another possible substitute chord for the ordinary dominant 7th. A note of caution, however: do not use the suspended 4th chord when the 3rd appears prominently in the melody. Below you will find a complete table of suspended 4th chords:

The Dominant 7th Chord with Suspended 4th

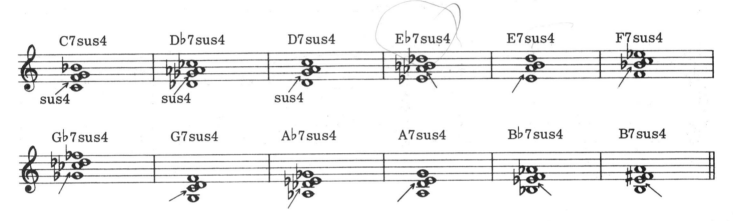

The Dominant 9th Chord with Suspended 4th

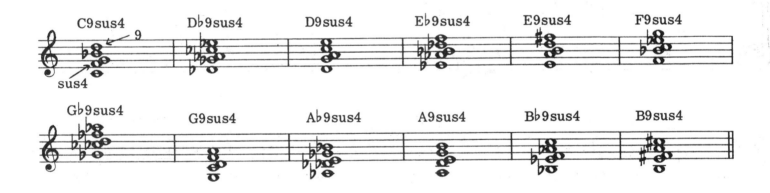

Best Voicings of the Dominant 9th Chord with Suspended 4th

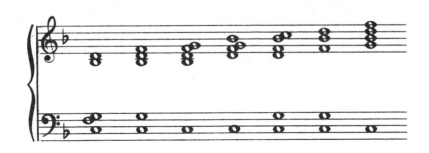

"Days of Wine and Roses" is a tender melody with a rich harmonization. Observe the use of 9ths, flatted 9ths, suspended 4ths and other altered chords all making for a rich musical sound. Analyze the chord structure and harmonization.

DAYS OF WINE AND ROSES

Words by
JOHNNY MERCER

Music by
HENRY MANCINI

This last section deals with 11th, 13th and altered chords used harmonically in full chord spelling or melodically in an improvisation.

Although 11th's and 13th's are not as commonly used as 9th or flatted 9th chords they add still another dimension in sound. Good jazz pianists use many 11th's and 13th's with altered tones, usually as substitutes for dominant 7th chords.

* * * * * * * * *

11th Chords

The following tables, will show the four most common types of 11th chords: the Major 11th, Dominant 11th, Augmented 11th and Minor 11th.

Major 11th Chords

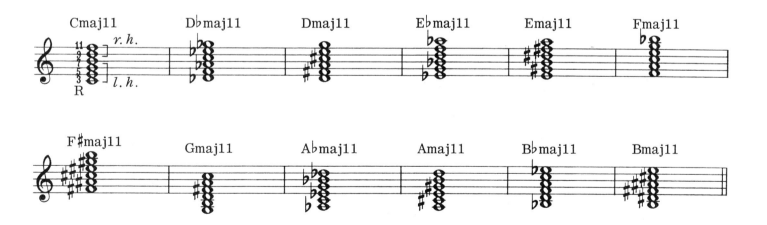

Editor's note: Omitting the 3rd of the above 11th chords will eliminate the harshness which some listeners find disturbing.

Dominant 11th Chords

Editor's note: This chord also sounds better with the 3rd omitted.

Augmented 11th Chords

Note: This chord is more commonly used than either the Major 11th or the Dominant 11th.

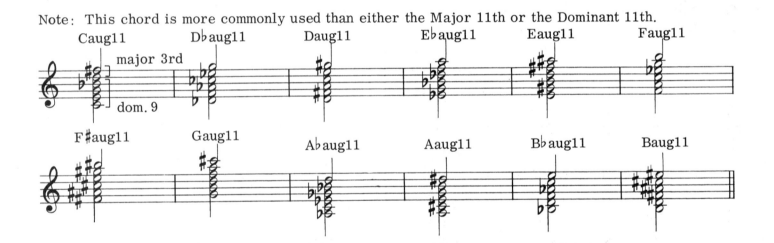

Minor 11th Chords

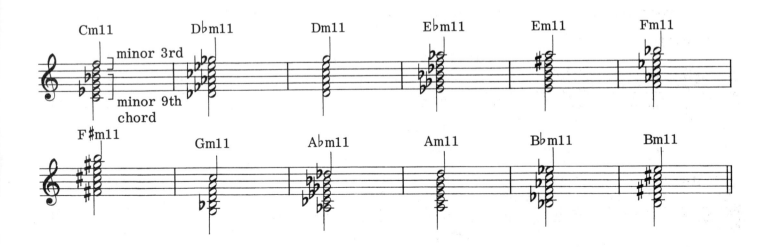

13th Chords

The two most commonly used 13th chords are 1) the Dominant 13th, and 2) the augmented 11th with the added 13th.

Dominant 13th Chords

(Symbol: 13)

FORMULA = DOMINANT 11th, PLUS MAJOR 3rd

C13 = C E G B♭ D F A

R 3 5 7 9 11 13

DOM. 11   maj. 3rd

DRILL: Spell dominant 13th chords on the following given root tones:

Editor's note: As in the case of the 11th chord, omit the third for a less dissonant sound.

Augmented 11th, added 13th Chords

(Symbol: 13+11 or 13aug11)

FORMULA = AUGMENTED 11th PLUS MINOR 3rd

Try your hand at filling out the following drill to form 13th chords with augmented 11ths.

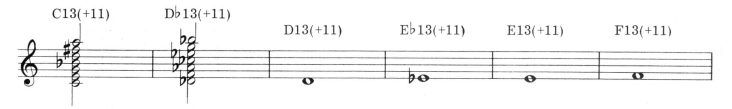

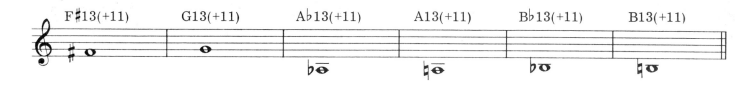

Bitonality

By this stage, we have extended the harmony to such a point that it has acquired a bitonal* quality.

Think of this formula as an easy way to find (for example) a C13+11

L. H. = C7 Dom.	R. H. = D major triad
C E G B♭	D F♯ A

or

I_7	II major

Thus the superimposition of the D major triad extends the C7 to a full 13th chord.

Other examples of chords which can be thought of as bitonal:

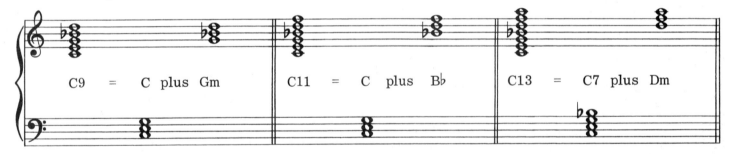

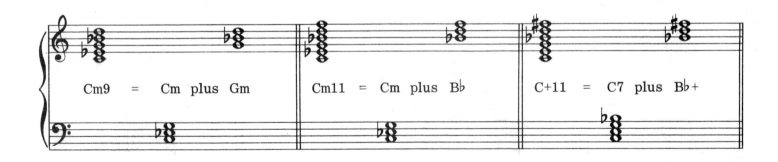

*Note: Bitonal = belonging to two different keys at the same time.

The Pedal Point

This is a wonderful device for building up excitement and tension in an arrangement. The pedal point is a tone which is repeated through a series of chords. The tone must belong to the first and last chords in the series, but need <u>not</u> belong to the other chords. Although the pedal point may appear in the melody or in an inner part, it is most commonly used in the bass. (See comments #4 and #5 below.)

* * * * * * * * * * * *

"A Time for Love" is a song harmonically rich in 9th, 11th, 13th and suspended 4th chords. Play it and listen to the sounds created by these extended harmonizations. All advanced chords have been analyzed. Note the following:

1) The 9th, 11th or 13th may be the melody note. (C13 chord in measure six.)

2) The 9th, 11th or 13th may be part of the harmonization. (A♭13 G♭ Bass measure 12.)

3) Sometimes chords are indicated as $\frac{6}{9}$. The 6th is technically the 13th of the chord and sometimes composers interchange these terms. (Note measure 3, B♭6$\left(\begin{smallmatrix}+7\\9\end{smallmatrix}\right)$. The note G which is the 6th of a B♭ chord is also the 13th. Here the composer chose to call it a 6th.)

4) The opening measures of the vocal line are a perfect illustration of a pedal point used in the bass. In measure 3, the bass note B♭ is the root of the B♭6$\left(\begin{smallmatrix}+7\\9\end{smallmatrix}\right)$ chord. In measure 4, the bass note B♭ is held—even though the chord changes to an A♭7. In measure 5, the B♭ bass once again becomes the root of the B♭ chord.

5) Note especially the use of the pedal point in the 9th measure. At first, the D bass note is the root of D9sus4; then it becomes the root of D7. Next however, it does <u>not</u> belong to the chord Am7(-5). The pedal point ends by becoming once again the root of D7.

A TIME FOR LOVE

12.05.99

Words by
PAUL FRANCIS WEBSTER

Music by
JOHNNY MANDEL

"Body and Soul" is presented as a complete arrangement and improvisation in parts; any altered or advanced chord spelling is analyzed and in several places substitute chords are used.

Study the chord alterations so that your own future arrangements may utilize this technique. Notice that the melodic improvisation often relies on the 9th, 11th and many times the 13th of the chord.

BODY AND SOUL

Words by
EDWARD HEYMAN, ROBERT SOUR
and FRANK EATON

Music by
JOHN GREEN

Working from a Lead Sheet

Most songs do not indicate 9, 11, or 13th chords. Consequently, it is up to the pianist to add these more exciting harmonies.

"April in Paris" is presented here with the chords and melody line in lead sheet form as you might find it in a "fake book." Try your hand at making your own arrangement of this beautiful song; add the more advanced chords whenever you can. . .

APRIL IN PARIS

Words by
E. Y. HARBURG

Music by
VERNON DUKE

676-2010

Sister Mary Margaret
Franciscan Rhythms

music Therapy
music Therapist

lessons from
Ken Vanhier } advanced
student
Classical & chord
study & improvisation

xanas
anxiety
relief

Info on schools
that teach it

what input
Start now?